RĀHU DAŚĀ

A Guide to Thrive

GARY O'TOOLE

Other Titles by Gary O'Toole

Cosmic Bodes: The Ayurvedic Astrology Guide to Health & Well-Being

Oṃ Gaṃ Gaṇapataye Namaḥ

Contents

There is a fine old story about a student who came to a rabbi and said, "In the olden days there were men who saw the face of God. Why don't they any more?" The rabbi replied, "Because nowadays no one can stoop so low."

- From Memories, Dreams, Reflections
by Carl Jung

Introduction

Rāhu is a shadow, the ascending lunar node that times the moment of an eclipse of the Sun or Moon. Thus, it has a dark quality. In India, it is called a 'shadow planet', along with the opposite descending lunar node, Ketu. While each person's experience of shadows is vastly different, there are some common themes we all experience. Some people work better in the shadows. Others may attempt to run away from parts of themselves they have long since shunned. But running away only gets you so far, as your shadow rears its head in the 18 years of Rāhu daśā, one of the nine planetary cycles that divide a person's life into chapters in Vedic astrology.

In those 18 years, Rāhu will make its way through each sign of the zodiac, transiting each for about 18 months. A shadow is cast over each area of your life as it does so, offering deeper insights but also obscuring each place. Rāhu is always extreme on either end of whatever spectrum you find yourself. There is a blocking of the light before you find it again. The darkness of this 'eclipse period' gives you the ability to see beyond what is presented on the surface; to evolve beyond what is. Ultimately, Rāhu, just as the eclipses, points to your evolution – whether you like it or not!

Western astrologers tend to speak of Rāhu in more positive terms, that it represents everything you ever wanted. While this is true, it is also your biggest block, what Indian astrologers refer to as *bādhaka*. It's both the block *and* the release, the darkness that leads to the light, the confusion that eventually leads to clarity.

As you journey through the zodiac during the 18 years of Rāhu daśā, you eventually transcend the false, shadow self, and move into the light of simply being upon entering Jupiter daśā, the subsequent time period. The clouds of confusion part and clarity returns once more. If you've been under a cloud of confusion for 18 years of Rāhu daśā, Jupiter's 'inner light', its inner knowing or intuition, is a return to sanity, to the truth of who you really are. It can be a profound shift in awareness. It's at least a comforting and reassuring return to sanity, a reconnection to something you probably lost during your Rāhu years.

Before you get back to the truth of who you are, you must become aware of all the masks you wear. Rāhu teaches you to be more authentic, but first it's probably going to make you feel like a fraud, an imposter. You're likely to fear exposing yourself, your shadow self, to others. But there's no side-stepping your shadow if you wish to become whole. You cannot ignore your shadow if you are to awaken to the truth of who you are.

To say that you have awakened suggests you must have been asleep for some time.

Rāhu is essentially a split that occurs in you. To recognise the split heals this division. How each person goes about this varies. Some may experience more extreme divisions which are labelled according to the help that is sought. Psychotic episodes may be a more extreme expression, but these may be labelled as a 'spiritual awakening' by others. Even if these kinds of extremes are not experienced, Rāhu still creates a split; between what is real and unreal; the person you put on show and the real you, hidden behind a mask. Yet you cannot simply drop the façade and function in society.

You must don many masks to achieve your ambitions. Being authentic all the time would not make you very popular! Yet Rāhu daśā asks you to go against the grain, against the natural flow of what society deems appropriate. You must go your own way, achieve your own goals, which may run counter to what others want from you. While you may never completely drop the pretence, the masks, or functional roles, Rāhu daśā is likely to highlight when and where hiding your true self, your whole self, no longer works for you.

You may live behind a persona you cannot free yourself from in public. But you are also more likely to project your repressed parts onto others who seem to display the traits you feel are inappropriate for you. A simple way to know what lies within your shadow is to look at what or who triggers you. This is your shadow rearing its head, rattling you to remind you it has been neglected, caged in the depths of your being. If only you were to listen to it, you could access so much more power within yourself. The fear of doing so is what keeps you held back. Without tapping into it, you cannot reach your full potential. As the saying goes, 'everything you want is beyond your fears'.

While Rāhu may represent many things for each individual, it is also a collective shadow we project onto others in mass movements and in different cultures. Whatever it represents for you personally, it shows the lengths you go to to find your truth. To find it, you must venture into far off lands in your mind, far from the reality of what is, so you can find new ways of being in the world. You may question each step of the way. Your mind may seem like a foreign land when Rāhu has a hold of you (Rāhu is one of the 9 *grahas* or 'graspers' of Vedic astrology). This journey is also full of wonder and excitement, too.

I know a little about this because I am coming to the end of my own 18-year Rāhu daśā as I write this. I've been there and worn the t-shirt many times. I've worn many t-shirts, each with a different trope; each an attempt to 'find myself'. I've come to realise I must take off the roles I've tried on, the many masks and 'functional shells.' I've come to realise the masks, the garbs, the roles, only serve to mask who I truly am, including the things I try to hide. Yet these are the things that make me who I am. While it's scary to show the real me, that's where Rāhu ultimately leads. It has shown me my shadow; mostly through experiences and behaviours of others I may have labelled inappropriate. Every challenging shadow encounter has been an opportunity for me to awaken to the wholeness of who I am.

Being truthful is about coming to terms with the truth of who we are, warts and all. This is what it means to be authentic. Yet many times we can see Rāhu-type behaviours as inauthentic and artificial. Rāhu is an imposter (we'll get to the myth of Rāhu later), and we're all imposters, really. We all pretend to 'be somebody'. This is a necessary part of playing roles in society. If we are to reach our full potential, we must 'fake it 'til we make it'.

If you are entering your own Rāhu daśā, get acquainted with your shadow, your blind spots, so you can live more authentically.

Oh, and get organised! If you did not read another sentence of this book, remember this, as Rāhu daśā tends to be at least a little chaotic. It can be a lot of fun, too. But just like a roller coaster, after a while you just want to get off.

As Rāhu daśā brings up your shadow, don't be afraid of this. Consciously bringing it into the light can only be an empowering experience. Yet you mustn't let the shadow impulses take you over either, as trying to satiate ever whim will only drain the life from you. Instead, use the impulse to tune into what has been neglected, incorporating it into your whole being.

Although I have not always explicitly referred to Ketu for much of the book, keep in mind that you cannot have a Rāhu experience without Ketu. They are two sides of the same coin. If Rāhu is experienced in a more constricted, compulsive way, it can lead to the opposite extreme, i.e., impulsiveness. Ketu can show impulsiveness. The more tempered Rāhu becomes, the more tempered Ketu is.

While anyone would benefit from reading a book that is about their shadow, those in Rāhu daśā will obviously benefit the most. Those with Rāhu as *Ātmakāraka* or 'soul planet' would benefit from consciously engaging with Rāhu. Your Ātmakāraka (soul significator) is the planet that has reached the highest degree in your birth chart. For Rāhu, the lower the degree, the higher it is, as it moves retrograde (backwards) through the signs. If you have Rāhu at a low degree, it may be your Ātmakāraka, offering you all the lessons contained within this book as major themes and soul lessons throughout your life. Be aware, however, that not all astrologers use Rāhu in this context. This is one of many controversial aspects related to the lunar nodes.

You would benefit greatly by calculating Rāhu's placement in your birth chart while reading this book. You should seek out a reputable resource when having your Vedic astrology chart calculated. Choose two or more resources to double-check the calculations if there are discrepancies. Make sure to verify the correct data before proceeding.

No One is Without Shadow

Rāhu is your blind spot. Whatever that is for you, whatever it rules (Aquarius is co-ruled by Rāhu) and wherever it is in your horoscope, it shows (or doesn't, I guess!) where you are at least somewhat unconscious. This unconscious part of you can create problems precisely because you are unaware. If you knew you were sabotaging yourself, you would more likely do something about it. If you're unwilling to accept your part in it, you're more likely to project this onto others.

Bādhaka

Vedic astrology has a term for Rāhu. It's called *bādhaka*, meaning 'block' or 'obstruction'. Rāhu is seen as co-ruler of Aquarius, along with Saturn, while modern Western astrologers say Uranus rules Aquarius. Uranus and Rāhu have much in common. They both represent surprise and innovation. And they both scare the hell out of us at times. They show an independent streak and revolutionary stance. They often reflect shocking events and shake-ups to the status quo. They change the current system and shake us out of unconscious behaviour. They do so by making us aware of where we have been asleep at the wheel.

Rāhu brings up blocks and fears to our evolution. But it does this so we can remove them. Aquarius is the natural 11th sign of the zodiac which, although ultimately about evolution and revolution, can actually create as many problems as it solves. In their book, *Coming Alive,* psychiatrists Barry Michels and Phil Stutz describe the shadow as "Part X", and how it creates "a problem you don't have to have and ... a solution that makes the problem worse." This is the problem with Rāhu and the sign Aquarius.

This concept can be a little confusing if you were to only view the 11th house as representing goals and gains. While it certainly is an area of life that shows gains, it also creates problems when we don't think about the long-term implications. Aquarius is as much about the unintended consequences of advancement as it is the advancement. This is where Saturn, the other ruler of Aquarius, the planet that shows you consequence, comes into play. Saturn could be said to represent the past, while Rāhu represents the future. We are often too eager to progress, creating problems for ourselves in the future which become the mistakes of our past.

The 11th house is the 6th from the 6th. The 6th house is the house of the enemy. And while the enemy of your enemy may be your friend, a signification of the 11th house, it can create more and more enemies, more and more problems to deal with on a larger scale. In other words, the more people you associate with, the more potential, for better or worse.

Would you trust someone without a shadow? Of course not! You would think they were a ghost. And indeed, Rāhu can make you feel like a ghost during its period, a poor imitation of what it is to be fully alive. But the other side of the coin is also possible. I've never felt so alive as I have in my own Rāhu years. It's like living on the razor's edge. If you enjoy intensity, you'll love it! Yet you may have to fall off the edge at times. I have, many times.

The higher you go, the lower you go.

You must get in touch with your shadow during

Rāhu daśā, if you are to avoid the pitfalls of projecting your shadow onto others who seem to coax you off the edge. This happens simply because you have not integrated your shadow and end up either hating others for achieving what you want, or seeing them as behaving inappropriately, doing the very things you were taught not to. Yet you cannot help but be intrigued by it. I've met enough people in their Rāhu daśā that have done things they never thought they were capable of to know this to be true. Though they may have viewed their behaviour as inappropriate, they eventually see how it led to their evolution.

When you call back your shadow projections, you become whole. That might sound nice, but what does it mean, exactly? Well, it means you experience a more balanced life and achieve more of what you want, when you realise where you hold back or deny certain parts of yourself that actually end up working against your best interest.

I didn't get this until about halfway through my own Rāhu daśā. Up to that point, I was constantly being challenged by others, being triggered in some way. I would continually meet people who would push my buttons. They often seemed to be doing so with some delight. They would challenge my authority, or ask endless questions, taking up more of my time than I had set out to give. They didn't seem to know what a healthy boundary looked like. Until I acknowledged this was all my doing, that it was I who didn't have proper boundaries, it could not change. As soon as I realised it was my hunger for more knowledge, my hunger for more of whatever, the problems I had with others began to fade. I no longer met people who challenged me as much. If I did, I would simply shrug it off and recognise it as my own doing. It didn't impact me as negatively. I could see it as a lesson I had to learn in setting healthy boundaries while also pushing them. A tricky balance to obtain but one that is possible. You are likely to have to learn the same lesson in your own way during Rāhu daśā. It becomes like a circus act you must master. But you cannot learn it by reading about it. You must learn it by living it.

It gets easier as soon as you acknowledge your own need to challenge others' boundaries, which is your shadow self challenging yours. You have caged this wild animal inside yourself and it's not happy until you acknowledge it.

We all have this wildness in different areas of our life. The more you can shine a light on the area you experience Rāhu, the more likely you can find a way to call back your projections. (See *Rāhu in Each Sign & House*).

The next time someone triggers you, investigate what was so triggering. What is it about them or their behaviour that rattled you?

While Jupiter is often referred to as 'The Great Protector', Rāhu may be called 'The Great Projector'. Rāhu and Jupiter are opposite in so many ways. Jupiter offers comfort, through people and things that offer a sense of meaning and connection. Teachers and advisers who soothe the soul are Jupiterian in nature. Jupiter has a protective role, insulating you from threats. And while there can be issues if there is too much comfort, and you never reach beyond your comfort zone, it's generally a force for good. Rāhu, on the other hand, challenges your boundaries and you are likely to feel unprotected and exposed as a result.

So, it's good to be aware of this and protect yourself to a degree. The problem with Rāhu daśā is being on the lookout for threat, constantly. It's worth noting that much of this hypervigilance is ill-placed in a modern context and, most likely, in your life. While it may have suited someone having to be vigilant for predators in the wilds in ancient times, you most likely don't need to protect yourself to that degree. This can lead to problems if you cannot shut off this response. You may feel like you are on constant altert, looking for how things could go wrong. At the same time, you must try many things that may indeed not work out, as Rāhu daśā is about innovation and change. So, your fear of failure is understandable. But the constant hypervigilance can be draining. See the chapter about *Antidotes* to counteract some of these tendencies.

Others may be aware of this when they meet you on some level. It's not conscious. They probably couldn't tell you why they feel stressed around you, but it's there. It's like when you meet with a vexed dog when you are afraid of dogs. It can sense your stress. Other people will sense something is off when you have unintegrated parts you project onto them. It's contagious.

The other side of this is you may feel drawn to people but cannot fathom why. They may fascinate you despite being outwardly repulsed by them. Or you may fall in love with someone you consciously think is trouble. This is your blind spot, Rāhu at work in your relationships. Whenever you feel inexplicably drawn to, or repulsed by, someone, this is your shadow banging on the cage, looking for attention. Give it some.

Life would be so much easier if we all were aware of our shadow projections, wouldn't it? But at least you cannot complain about Rāhu daśā being boring! Rāhu daśā is rarely so, which is actually one of the problems. The impulse is to constantly push the envelope, to constantly push yourself to evolve. The problem is you are likely to do so too quickly. It's usually too much, too soon. By doing so, you are unlikely to integrate all your more exaggerated experiences. Recognising you are at the helm, on some level, helps. But it doesn't necessarily stop the intensity, an intensity you are asking for, whether you realise it or not. You must learn to manage it, while acknowledging your need for it. And if you don't find yourself on high alert, you may experience a sort of constant low-grade anxiety. People you meet are likely to elicit a strong response in you, whether positive or negative. Rāhu knows no boundaries. It can be fear-inducing but exhilarating at the same time, just like a roller coaster.

The good news is that this is an opportunity to transform, a catalyst that kick starts a process of evolution, a quantum leap. But don't expect it to be a walk in the park. If it were that easy, you would have done so prior to Rāhu daśā.

You cannot have an experience that is not in your horoscope. Everyone and everything in your life is in your birth chart. Although Rāhu is your biggest blind spot, it is still part of you. Why not embrace it, so you can make the most of it all?

Some may be more attuned to their unconscious or have worked on what they perceive as only bad qualities they have repressed; that they may actually repress their light, their positive qualities. These can be projected onto others as much as the darker material. If, for example, you think you're not good enough to accomplish a feat, and watch someone doing what you think you cannot, because you don't feel you have the required skills or confidence, you may project onto them your greatest hidden talents. If a strong envy is stirred in you, it's worth paying attention to it. Your shadow may get triggered by their abilities because your shadow is a part of you that knows you can do it. Yet you have repressed this because others may have told you that you couldn't, perhaps because of their own fears. Fear is contagious. And, while a certain amount of caution is healthy, oftentimes it may become a crippling anxiety. So don't simply think of your shadow as harbouring only darker qualities that you must keep away from society. It contains all your power you may be too afraid to acknowledge.

Mostly, however, you are likely to repress thoughts and feelings you have deemed to be unsuitable to fit into society. Rāhu daśā comes at a time in your life when these realisations are ripe, expressing themselves in people and events that reveal your shadow. It's likely to make you feel like an outsider, so you can engage with the forgotten parts of yourself. You can see this as an opportunity to explore your hidden depths, the things you could not do with the usual people around you. When surrounded by people who are not your usual mix, or in countries or places you previously had not visited, you can explore different parts of yourself, including your shadow.

If you're not under the scrutiny of others who think about you a certain way, keeping you caged, you can experiment with other ways of being in the world. This is one of the gifts of Rāhu daśā. It's an opportunity to evolve. Yet you may need to go it alone as you do so. You're likely to feel cast adrift, lost at sea, at times. Certain groups and relationships need to adjust, or you will find yourself being ostracized by them. Don't just look at doors that are closing, look at what is opening up for you to experience on your own. At the same time, try not to alienate yourself. You need others' support as you try different things out for yourself.

Have one foot in and one foot out, as it were. This may mean assimilating within the group outwardly, but inwardly delving into what you truly stand for, apart from others' opinions of you. You could do with some comfort from familiar friends and family while you explore what is possible. Yet you must feel free to try something else, something which may be against others' wishes. This is a balancing act you must master. Decipher who or what needs to go, keeping those around you who allow you to express the full gamut of your potential, including parts of you that may seem strange or inappropriate. Don't just view this departure from the norm as bad news; see it as an opportunity to explore yourself, including all those thoughts and feelings you had to repress to fit in.

Use being triggered by others' behaviour to find out what you are truly about. If you deplore shoddy work and pride yourself on making great pieces of art every time you do something, your shadow could be a shoddy and unkempt part you've long since rejected. If you are outwardly a perfectionist and meet someone like this, they are likely to rub you up the wrong way. You may complain about their ineffectual and messy work practices but fail to see this is something buried deep within yourself, a part of you that was repressed early on for whatever reason. It may have been a parent or teacher that taught you that shoddy work is unacceptable, even though there may be a part of you that enjoyed being a messy creator, as children often are. Or, you may have seen how such behaviour was frowned upon by society. Rāhu daśā is an opportunity to mess up for a while. You are finding your own unique way of doing things. If you've never tried something before, it's likely you mess up for a time.

You must still live within society, of course, but you must explore other parts of you if you are to incorporate these and become whole. In the end, you can actually become a more productive member of society.

This is just one example. You could substitute this with anything you deem inappropriate in another. Just look for what triggers you in others. If you don't like when someone turns up late, or you see them as too shallow, or too emotional, whatever it may be, this is your shadow, the part of you you could do with at least looking at.

By calling back your projections, you integrate these and maintain your integrity. By failing to do so, you continue to meet with people and events that challenge you to wake up to all of you.

You may become the 'black sheep' during Rāhu daśā. If you already identify with Rāhu all along, Rāhu daśā is likely to accentuate this tendency. Even if you do not usually identify with being the odd one out, you are likely to get involved in unusual experiments during Rāhu daśā, meeting people you deem to be unusual, or those from a foreign culture. You may not have built up an immunity to the downsides of such exposure. You are likely to feel challenged. Whatever you feel about it, the experience of different people and circumstances helps you to evolve.

Rāhu daśā shows a hidden desire (perhaps even hidden from you) to do something different. You must go it alone on this journey. There are many advantages, and some disadvantages, beyond the more obvious disadvantages of going it alone. Keeping unusual hours or doing things your own way may mean you may find yourself driving against the flow of rush hour traffic. You may actually do things better than anyone else. If you work for a company, you're likely to bring some new ideas to the table. They may not be received well initially or at all.

I kept unusual hours during Rāhu daśā, but I took full advantage of it. I didn't run with the pack and sought out different perspectives. The downside of going it alone is you may feel lost on your own, of course. If you're not running with the pack, it can be a very isolating experience. Social interaction keeps us feeling safe and connected. At the very least, you may question what you are doing. Others are unlikely to be on board with what you are doing. You are threatening to them. Best to write whatever insights you have and offer it in a way they can digest later.

If you try to force your insights on others, confronting them and challenging them, you are likely to experience a backlash. But then, I would ask you: Who on earth has created innovation on this planet without experiencing a backlash? If you haven't, it may be that you are not facing up to your full potential. You may hold back through fear, but you can only hold the dam back for so long.

I once asked my astrology teacher, Pearl Finn, if it were possible 'to do Rāhu' without stepping on other people's toes. There was no hesitation in her answer: No!

Out there on the cutting edge, you are likely to feel

at least some doubt about what you are doing, especially if you are pushing things too far, too quickly. Pace yourself. You won't have everyone else at your back. You need to practice being on the leading edge of whatever you are doing. Living authentically may mean rubbing a lot of people up the wrong way. In our conversations on the *Timeline Astrology Podcasts*, Jeanette 'Kishori' McKenzie reminds me to place my hand on my heart, to "dwell in the Heartfield." You can incorporate this simple centering gesture into your life, too (see the chapter on *Antidotes* for more remedial measures).

On a walk in the woods, I once came across a tree that stood out from the rest. It had literally turned grey in colour (Rāhu is often depicted as 'smoky' in colour in Vedic astrology). It was out on its own, on the cutting edge, and feeling the separation. It was quite a striking sight. You must do the same during Rāhu daśā. You must step out on your own and discover your own way. You will be striking to behold. Embrace your power to stand out.

Prior to my own Rāhu daśā, I don't think I ever thought about achieving anything of significance in my life. I had ambitions, don't get me wrong. When I was young, I aspired to 'be somebody'. But nothing like when Rāhu daśā began. Rāhu is in Sagittarius in my chart. I have been chasing down knowledge throughout

Rāhu daśā as if it has an expiration date. Rāhu's ambition is a bottomless pit. No matter how much I've achieved in the 18 years of Rāhu daśā, I never thought it was enough. The reason? I didn't think I was enough. In doing so, I have learned I am enough, just as I am.

Rāhu makes us all think this way; in a way that makes us feel like we are seperate. But here's the thing; you have to go through it, to come out the other end, realising you are enough, just as you are. Nothing is needed. You don't need to prove yourself, your worth, to anyone. But before you get there, you are probably going to give it a good try.

The insatiable desire to 'be somebody' began to wane in and around the last third of the major cycle, when the Rāhu-Sun sub-period kicked in (more on this in the chapter, *Nine Phases of Rāhu Daśā*). I slowly came to the realisation that being somebody, achieving some success, being ambitious, is the most disconnecting experience. This experience usually peaks in Rāhu-Sun. It usually plays out as the need to be recognised by others, when in fact, the truth of Rāhu-Sun is the need to find oneself. When you do that, you are successful. Anything else is a pale imitation of success.

To be worldly successful, as is often the need in Rāhu-Sun, you often have to step over others to get there, thinking yourself to be different to them, separate to them. I was never comfortable with that. I always wanted to help others. But I've had to acknowledge my need for achievement, too. You will no doubt experience this dichotomy on some level in Rāhu daśā.

In the past decade, I've written three books, including this one (I never thought I had even one book in me), produced a podcast series and magazine, and built a client base. I've achieved a great deal more than I thought myself capable of. Yet it's not enough. And it never will be. No matter how much you get with Rāhu, it's never enough.

The Pursuit of Happiness

Here's the thing: You want to have a goal you can never attain in Rāhu daśā. You need something you can keep chasing. You may end up feeling as if you are chasing your tail, of course, but you can always see the chase as just that, a chase. Rāhu daśā is about the chase, not about what you are chasing. But here's the other thing: By chasing–anything–you are actually telling yourself you don't have that thing. You must, however, continue to chase and see it as a means to teach you an important lesson: There is nothing out there that can complete you. It's all an inside job.

You can make the chase a game for yourself, especially once you realise it doesn't matter whether you get what you want or not. It's about waking up to this profound truth while continuing to move forward.

Rāhu is about novelty, always looking for something new. If it's not new, or a new way you have of approaching something familiar, it's not going to satisfy you in Rāhu daśā. It's not going to satisfy you, anyway, but at least you understand the need for novelty and can do it while seeing what it's teaching you about yourself.

Rāhu is, in a way, the reason you're here in a bodysuit in the first place, the desire your soul had for something it did not experience before. It's also the realisation that the impulse to be born, to be somebody, is the same impulse that creates so many problems for you while still in physical form. If you are somebody, something specific, you close yourself off to be anything. You restrict the flow of the universe when you try to "pigeonhole" yourself, cutting off something that is trying to make its way to you. In Rāhu daśā, the route is through the back door, as it were, through your shadow.

You may resist change that is necessary for your evolution, or you might change too much too soon. In striving for something you do not have, it creates a sense of separation, which reinforces your perception of being alone, your otherliness. Whether you reach your ultimate goal, or fail to achieve any, you end up feeling stuck. You may not realise it's actually not about the goal, but the journey to wholeness in your search for your disparate parts that's important. On the other hand, if you never reach your goals, at least you can continue striving. Problems begin when you achieve everything you thought you ever wanted and still feel lack, a hunger for more.

We can blame one particular neurochemical for all of this: dopamine. This is what gets you out of bed in the morning. But satiate ever little whim and every dream you ever had and see what that does for you. You're unlikely to feel so enthusiastic. When you do anything to excess, dopamine floods your system and the things that used to bring you pleasure no longer do. It has to be novel. You may end up with addictions; addiction to success; to material things; to substances, whatever. Whatever took the edge off initially, when done to excess (be it sex, drugs, success, whatever) no longer hits the spot.

There's a common misconception about what dopamine does. Dopamine is *not* about the thing you want. It's about the pursuit. Once you get something you thought you always wanted, you're left with not one but two more problems. You already had the problem of not having what you wanted, but now you replaced it with two more: 1) you got what you wanted but so what, it's not what you thought it would be, and 2) you now don't have something to strive for.

We all need something beyond us, either just beyond our capabilities, or beyond us as individuals, to strive towards. We need something bigger than us as individuals, something more meaningful than our selfish pursuits. Even if we have all our desires met, we need even bigger ones. But then, where does it end? It doesn't, of course. At least, not during Rāhu daśā. Rāhu's want is a bottomless pit.

There's one thing I learned to cultivate in Rāhu daśā as much as possible, although this is not its natural mode. You can, too. I trained myself to measure myself from where I came from, to where I was, as much as possible. The default for Rāhu is to look ahead, to measure yourself from where you are to where you want to be. But if you do that, you will always be left wanting.

The pursuit of happiness is actually telling yourself you are not happy, that you don't have what you want. That kind of want is horrible. And, in a way, it's not the point. The point is, you have already asked for what you want, consciously or not. It's the block to getting it that you may not have addressed. You haven't addressed Rāhu, your shadow, where you feel contracted, all twisted up about what you don't have. Once you undo that knot, you can achieve anything, as and when 'all of you' is on board. And yet, feeling unfulfilled is actually part of the journey to wholeness in Rāhu daśā. You cannot bypass this step. If you don't address your shadow, it behaves in ways that actually work against what you want deep down. It plays havoc with your life by throwing temptations in your way, every step of the way. Even the most disciplined eventually give in and indulge an impulse that actually drains. Whereas, if you were to take it on, it could fuel you.

Another tendency I've spotted in myself in Rāhu daśā is the tendency to leave things to the last minute. Although I was not consciously doing this, I know why I was unconsciously setting this up. I was doing it for the thrill and excitement of the chase, dashing around trying to get things done at the very last minute. Rāhu is a rush of adrenaline. Add that to the surge in dopamine. If you keep it up for long periods, it's hard to switch off. This is why many people end up with chronic mental and/or physical conditions in Rāhu daśā, especially if Rāhu were in a place that impacted health. Even without impacting health in a direct way, Rāhu daśā can do so indirectly, by always 'being on'. It can feel like a roller coaster. After a while you cannot shut off, even when the ride has come to a stop.

I may be stepping off this ride, but my world is still spinning. It takes a while to decompress.

If I had this or that, I'd be happy, you tell yourself. But when you get this or that, you want more. You realise that's not it. Happiness is just a state of mind; it's fleeting. On the other hand, you always have access to an inner joy that is not based on outer experience. And you have access to something even greater: a meaningful purpose. If you have a purpose in life, you'll overcome any temporary thought or emotion to see it through. It's bigger than you. And you develop an inner joy when you do it. This is the key to unlocking the problems of Rāhu daśā.

We're all born with a gaping hole. That hole is Rāhu.

We attempt to fill it with stuff, with experiences, but these don't work. And yet, you must chase them to learn this lesson. You cannot skip this step.

Some commentators refer to three reasons the pursuit of happiness actually makes us miserable. These are comparison, self-centeredness, and overthinking.

Rāhu is all about comparing yourself to others, or to where you wish to be and will never be. It's about comparing yourself to those who have what you want; something that you apparently don't have. It doesn't matter if you are the head of a multibillion-dollar corporation or someone who hasn't been able to get a job; this type of comparison leads to the same feelings of unfulfillment.

Rāhu makes you self-centered. That's obvious and not so obvious in equal measures. You see, Rāhu is the imposter self, not the true Self. Yet it can trick its way in. You may think that role or position is your true self, but eventually, it falls away and reveals an empty shell. The Sun represents a healthy sense of self and self-esteem. Rāhu is a shadow that is cast, an artificial self.

Overthinking it can also swing wildly to the opposite extreme, when you've exhausted all sense and reason; that is, complete and utter unconscious, reckless behaviour. The more extreme thinking becomes, the more extreme its opposite must be. The more you overdo anything, the more the opposite must become extreme to compensate. Nature is always looking for balance. If you do anything to extreme, it will find it by giving you the other extreme.

The higher you go, the lower you go.

The opposite of Rāhu's obsessive drive to experience something is not satisfaction; it's annihilation. The opposite of running towards something is running away from it. This is represented by Ketu, the south node's more extreme guise. The more tempered Rāhu becomes, the more tempered Ketu becomes. Eventually, they can meet in the middle, where there is not just a sense of satisfaction, but a sense of fullness, of Beingness. You realise that the emptiness you feel, when faced fully, is actually full – of everything. You have everything you need, right now.

It may take some time for you to have this realisation, of course. In the meantime, you must go with it. Rāhu is primal. Don't try to fight it. Put on your fake smile and pay the heavy price of covering up your desires. The more you fight with your demons, the more they win. I am not suggesting letting yourself fall into any and all temptations that you stumble upon. What I am suggesting is you search high and low, to become familiar with your shadow.

The lower you go, the higher you go.

High in this context does not mean a dopamine fix. It means to connect with something higher, within.

Philosopher and writer Ken Wilber has so many truths to share about the shadow. He speaks about the need to "transcend and include." This describes how the process of evolution should occur; that is, you must transcend your current reality to a degree, but include where you are coming from as you progress. But it's tricky. If you evolve too quickly, you end up with undigested experiences that clog your system. This is why Rāhu also represents the blocks (bādhaka) you face.

Rāhu is your fear, but it can swing to the other side of fearlessness, even recklessness. Rāhu is a survival instinct. When you feel threatened, no matter how untrue or unreal the threat, you act out of fear of lack. It doesn't matter if you have all the comforts the world could provide; it does not remove this primal fear of lack. If Rāhu correlates with dopamine, and you get what you always thought you wanted only to feel empty inside, you may indeed sabotage that very thing, so you can continue the chase.

Now, go to your birth chart and see where you have probably done this many times. If Rāhu is in your 7th house of relationships, this may mean jumping into relationship after relationship that don't seem to work out. It's all working out brilliantly from your shadow's perspective. Rāhu in the 4th? No matter how much you think you are happy, there's another thought you are not. When you get the perfect setting, the perfect home, you'll end up sabotaging it, even if only in your mind, so you can chase it again.

I have Rāhu in the 2nd house of food and finances. I've been on a quest to fill my belly a lot in Rāhu daśā. I've been obsessed about food, to make me feel a certain way (Rāhu rules my 4th house Aquarius), so the analogy of not being satiated is not lost on me. I've also been through a bankruptcy in Rāhu daśā. Rāhu is in Sagittarius in my birth chart, so I've been more obsessed with acquiring knowledge than anything else. But no matter how much I get, it's not satisfying. It's not about the thing; it's about the chase. "But," I can hear you say, "I didn't ask for this." Rāhu is unconscious, remember. It is shadow, i.e., a hidden 'part' of you that has asked for it on some level. Not the 'you' you think of as you, and not just your shadow, within the context of the larger part or deeper existential 'non-part' of you that has chosen everything before the small you arrived on the scene.

So, what about the person who lives with a chronic illness for their entire Rāhu daśā?

I've seen many chronic conditions rear their head in people's lives during their Rāhu daśā. No one would consciously choose it. Yet someone with Rāhu in the 6th or 8th house of the horoscope, for example, is likely to experience something in that domain. Someone with Rāhu in the 6th or 8th may experience something minor or a debilitating illness, depending on the specifics of their birth chart. One thing is apparent in all cases: a fascination with whatever Rāhu impacts. Rāhu in the 6th may simply mean an obsession with perceived enemies and competition, Rāhu in the 8th as an obsession with trauma. If this is taken to the extreme, you may find yourself worse for wear, even if you do not end up with an illness.

The shadow 'part' of you is fascinated by it, whatever "it" is, thus attracting the issue into your life over and over. But you're unlikely to admit it because you may not even be aware of your shadow. Conscious awareness of this is the best way out of the conundrum.

Rāhu is a bottomless pit. But it doesn't mean you're not going to try to fill it. Actually, that's what most of Rāhu daśā is about. You probably have all you could ever need, so Rāhu daśā is more about constantly (unconsciously) shaking things up. If you're well-established entering Rāhu daśā, it's likely you are going to sabotage this unconsciously, so you can chase it again.

Four Aims of Life

Your experience of Rāhu will depend on the sign and house or place it's in, in your birth chart, and by transit, as well as the planet which rules these signs. Rāhu impacts certain areas based on the four aims in life. The four aims of life according to Vedic thought are *dharma, artha, kāma* and *mokṣa*. These Sanskrit terms represent four important directions of life: duty, work, pleasure, and release.

You can easily find which aims are more prominent in your life by counting how many planets are in each house in your birth chart. Rāhu in each house tends to distort the aim and make it harder to hit the target.

When you have Rāhu in either of the artha houses, 2, 6 or 10, you are likely to focus a lot on issues with family and finances (2); work and healthy routines, as well as competition (6); and career or social status (10). If you were not challenged by the competition, or a health issue, you are unlikely to make improvements. Rāhu will ultimately improve your lot in any of these areas, but usually through some sort of problem you must overcome. The extent to which it causes problems depends on the sign position, as well as the position of the sign's ruling planet (more on this later).

When Rāhu is in any of the kāma houses, 3, 7 or 11, it can show selfish desires (3) that may not be satisfied with just one person (7) or goal in life (11). You may sabotage a relationship, be it a friend or lover, to chase another. You may reach your goals but are unsatisfied with what you have achieved. You are not likely conscious of doing so, of course. Rāhu is your blind spot.

If you have Rāhu in any of the mokṣa houses, 4, 8 or 12, the desire for contentment (4), transcendence (8) and ultimate liberation (12) can be tricky because to be content means not needing anything; the desire to transcend worldly matters can keep you tied to what you wish to be free from, while true liberation means being free of all desire. Rāhu brings up a lot of desire. Desire and liberation are a tricky combination because you must yearn for nothing to be truly liberated.

Rāhu in the dharma houses, 1, 5 or 9, is even trickier because the truth of who you are (1), who you are becoming (5) and the traditions you follow (9), can get muddled in Rāhu's divergent path. You may not be satisfied with the tradition you were born within. You may sidestep tradition in Rāhu daśā, either moving country, changing jobs or the way you work, or changing cultures or religion. While this may lead to invaluable insights, it's just as likely to leave you feeling left in the dark and unclear as to what you believe to be true. No matter how insightful your lone journey is, you are on your own when it comes to figuring it all out.

Whether it's a dead end or peak experience, it may not matter in the grand scheme of things. Rāhu brings you to the same end result. It brings you back to clarity about who you truly are, beyond all the failed attempts and successes of this world.

I sometimes ask my astrology clients who are experiencing Rāhu daśā the question: "What is worse: Not getting what you want, or getting everything you ever wanted?" Those who have been through some years of Rāhu daśā often smile in recognition. In the end, both bring the same result; that is, a dissatisfaction that leaves you looking for something beyond all the success and failures.

Their smile of recognition is a light being shone where only their shadow lay for some time. Or as one commentator on one of my recent posts put it, "Feels like you just handed me a key to a golden door." To get the key, you must first meet the dragon, as Kishori speaks of in our conversations about Rāhu. There's no way around it. In the end, you wouldn't want it any other way.

Your life is your unique path, and no one can live it for you. Discovering where you may be more imbalanced, overemphasizing one over another, can help you live a more wholistic life, where all your needs are met. You can become whole after you experience the split.

Six Weaknesses of Mind

There are six weaknesses, or 'enemies', of the mind according to Vedic thought that come from a false sense of self and attachment. These are greed, arrogance, anger, attachment, lust and jealousy. These mental weaknesses can be seen to correlate with Rāhu and Ketu, Saturn, Mars, Venus, and Mercury more so, although the Sun, Moon, and Jupiter can play a role in each.

Sun, Moon, and Jupiter may not directly show these weaknesses if they are strong in your birth chart, as they are seen as pure and balanced. Yet even then, Sun, Moon, or Jupiter conjoined Rāhu, infected by greed, can show issues. Rāhu blocks the light of the Sun and Moon, and the 'inner light' and intelligence of Jupiter, from functioning optimally.

Rāhu conjoined the Sun can easily slip into arrogance, especially if the Sun itself were inflated in exaltation in Aries, Mars' sign, or deflated in Libra, Saturn's sign of exaltation. An inflated ego is more obviously seen with the Sun in Aries, but this can also be expressed as an overcompensation for a sense of lack when the Sun is in Libra.

Anger may also express itself through a Rāhu-Sun combination, especially if in a sign like Aries and you don't feel you are getting the recognition you think you deserve.

Rāhu conjoined the Moon can bring fear into the mind and can inflate other weaknesses such as greed, lust or anger. A debilitated Moon in Mars' sign Scorpio, conjunct Rāhu, may deplete the mental faculties and bring bitterness at the sense of loss. While this may not be outwardly expressed as anger, it may be expressed as an internalised rage, felt as depression.

Rāhu conjoined Jupiter can challenge calmness and coherence. Rāhu's greediness can spoil the generosity of Jupiter. Rāhu and Jupiter can combine to show even more greed if Jupiter is ill-disposed and lacks strength. Or it may show false hope and too much idealism, leading the person astray. A person may be greedy because of a lack of faith, leading to a lack of generosity. Someone may need to feel more financially secure, for example, before they are willing to share. Even then, the purity of Jupiter, expressed in altruism, can be tainted in some way by Rāhu. Ultimately, this can lead to loss, as greed always does. Even if you don't personally experience loss, someone is losing out.

Greed

Greed is troublesome. Unconscious greed is even more so. It can spoil even the best of situations. You may have an unconscious drive for something you are not conscious of, even if it's a problem for you as well as others. But it matters not whether the need is wholesome; greed always leads to problems in the end.

Wherever Rāhu sits in your birth chart shows where you are greedy. This will also impact the planet that rules the sign, as well as planets it is with or influencing by aspect. Rāhu is seen as influencing (aspecting) the same elemental signs. So, if Rāhu were in the water sign Cancer, it would influence the other water signs, Scorpio, and Pisces. It is also said to cast an aspect and influence on the sign it has just left by transit. Thus, it influences the 12th house from itself counting in retrograde motion, or the 2nd sign counting zodiacally. The mean calculation of Rāhu always transits backwards through the signs, whereas the true calculation can show it stationing direct at times.

Planets Rāhu associates with, either by conjunction or rulership of the sign, are impacted by greed in one way or another. It may not be obvious, as nothing about Rāhu is, but you may end up with problems when the greed for more creates more problems. More resources may not seem like a problem initially, but eventually leads to issues. Eating too much food is an obvious example (Rāhu in 2nd house). But unconscious greed for something you would not consciously choose is likely to show up as a problem a lot quicker. You may have more problems in general with Rāhu in the 6th, 8th, or 12th houses, for example.

This may be through an ongoing experience, as and when someone is born when Rāhu is conjoined a planet or in a certain house, or a temporary experience during a transit. Each of the planets, Saturn, Mars, Venus, and Mercury, represent most of our weaknesses, while the exaggerated Rāhu increases these weaknesses all the more.

Arrogance

Saturn or the Sun can show arrogance. Rāhu exaggerates and inflates the ego and can be seen as Saturn's alter-ego, further inflating arrogance, which shows you have further to fall. Arrogance disconnects you from the reality of life, just like ambition. If you are arrogant, you are unlikely to realise the bigger picture and truth of who you are. You are cutting yourself off from others through your arrogance and ambition. It eventually leads to a letdown, especially during the Rāhu-Saturn sub-period, which may challenge you to be humble if you are more prone to this weakness.

If Rāhu combines with Saturn, they combine in

such a way that it leaves you perched on a dangerous ledge. You may have great ambitions (Rāhu), yet you also have to do the responsible thing (Saturn). It may be a challenge to manage your expectations. It is, however, serving a greater purpose; that is, to let you know you are 'not all that' and are humbled. Sun inflated in Aries conjoined Rāhu, or deflated in Libra, shows some extreme expression that can flip to its opposite. You may be extremely arrogant or pretend to 'be somebody', but eventually must eat some humble pie. Until you learn to be more giving and humbler, both antidotes to Rāhu-Saturn and Rāhu-Sun, you are likely to have problems.

Rāhu and Saturn co-rule Aquarius as per Vedic astrology, which is at least one thing they have in common. They are both said to represent the air element, which Aquarius is dominant in. Yet the experience of air through Rāhu or Saturn is very different. Saturn can show a very necessary detachment in order to work hard at a long-term goal (Aquarius), while Rāhu can exaggerate detachment to the point of being completely removed from reality. If Saturn were a cool breeze, Rāhu can feel like a hurricane, completely distorting your perceptions about reality.

One of the things Rāhu and Saturn do have in common is ambition. While ambition requires a certain detachment, of course, a detachment from immediate gratification, it may also detach you from what is real. The more ambitious you are, the more disconnected you are from what is happening now. Instead, it focuses you on what you want in the future.

Aquarius is a future-oriented sign, as represented by Rāhu. This is also why it's one of the more complex signs, as Saturn represents the past. Neither is present to the reality of the moment. If you are stuck in the past, sad about your failures, or projecting into the future, and what may be, you are not experiencing the reality of the present moment. There's a certain arrogance implied here. Yet you could also use what has happened to you in the past to evolve. And you could do so while being focused on the present moment, including all of what is to achieve what may be – humbly.

Anger

Mars represents the courage to destroy the things that make you feel weak. When Mars is afflicted by Rāhu, a person may feel blocked in overcoming their weaknesses, or may overcompensate and push harder than is necessary. In doing so, they may create more problems, not knowing when to quit. Mars is your two-year-old self, stomping his or her feet when you don't get your way. Rāhu can block Mars from expressing itself clearly. Eventually, it explodes, or implodes, potentially leading to harm.

Most people are uncomfortable with their anger, but more so when it comes to other people's. This becomes even more of a problem when the shadow of

Rāhu is involved. Someone may project their anger onto others who seem aggressive. Others may say they are simply good at getting what they want. Any kind of discomfort with other people's anger may be rattling your two-year-old self in its shadowy cage.

Mars reflects our ego's need for self-protection, while Rāhu exaggerates and distorts the sense of self and the sense of threat. If someone feels others are not paying attention to them; or worse still, they seem to be deliberately obstructing, they may get angry. The natural impulse of Mars is to simply state your case: "I need to have this, and I need it now." However, because we are taught from a very early age to suppress what we want all the time, most of us have an innate problem with getting what we want all the time.

Rāhu can block Mars from expressing itself clearly, disturbing the individual's potential and experience of willfulness. Someone with a Rāhu-Mars connection may experience extreme highs and lows in their energy and output. If something doesn't make them scared, it will make them angry. Anger has its root in fear, of course. Both Rāhu and Mars represent a self-protective mechanism which usually creates more problems than it solves.

A Rāhu-Mars combination, either Rāhu in Aries or Scorpio, or in a conjunction with Mars, is likely to bring up issues of greed and bitterness when not having one's needs met. Someone may get angry when they don't get what they want and lash out at others who are perceived to be denying them. They may feel challenged to do something but take the impulse too far and actually block the very thing they want. If there's one thing Rāhu and Mars have in common, it's not knowing when to quit!

Whenever a planet gets together with Rāhu, it takes on some of its qualities, including its backwards or retrograde nature. Martin Schulman writes in his book, *Karmic Astrology: Retrogrades and Reincarnation* (Schulman 1977), of three distinct phases of retrogrades. He highlights the three phases in relation to retrograde planets as:

1. Jumping ahead of himself trying to live the future now,
2. In the process of living out the future, experiencing the feelings that he has already been there,
3. Repeating in mind the first phase, so that he is actually reliving the looking forward to a future that has already occurred.

It becomes a case of thinking back to looking forward to what has already happened! If you are constantly anticipating threats from the future, when something does happen, you have less energy to deal with problems effectively when they do come along. Rāhu blocks Mars from operating in its purest form, distorting the will into defending a self that is not real, making up problems that are not real, and coming up with solutions that are not helpful.

Someone with Rāhu-Mars combined in some way may deny the impulse initially, but then jump impulsively into actions they spend a lot of time regretting. Even if you are able to channel it in a healthy way, other people are not comfortable with your anger and may try to shut you down. If your anger is inappropriate or a threat, this may indeed be warranted. Taken to the extreme, rage may be expressed, although usually Rāhu-Mars is only harmful to oneself.

Lust

Venus and the Moon lust. Throw Rāhu into the mix and you have a situation where someone may feel nothing is satisfying, no matter the extremes of pleasure.

A Rāhu-Venus combination, either Rāhu in Taurus or Libra, or a Rāhu-Venus conjunction or time period, can throw up all kinds of complex issues around desire and attraction. Greed and lust combined can show that nothing and no one is ever enough. Someone may feel unsatisfied and continually chase a high that eventually feels more and more unfulfilling. The more extreme the pleasure, the more intense the pain, as one counteracts the other.

As high as you go is as low as you go.

If you are partnered in a Rāhu-Venus period, without any other mitigating factors, you may not appreciate your partner or feel appreciated by them. You may seek out others to fill an apparent void. Yet no amount of indulgence is going to cut it. Rāhu-Venus is a time to instead realise it's not enough to have experiences, there must be something more meaningful and purposeful behind whatever it is you do, whomever you do it with. You may indeed attempt to satisfy some elusive sense or craving for something other. Rāhu-Venus reflects a sense of the 'grass is always greener'. Knowing the futility of this on some level, it doesn't stop you trying to find something or someone else.

Greed and lust combine with Rāhu-Venus or Rāhu-Moon in all kinds of ways that you may or may not be conscious of. The most extreme, darker quality of Rāhu-Venus is sexual assault. It may at least show a lack of healthy boundaries around sexual intimacy. Rāhu-Venus or Rāhu-Moon may show someone taking advantage of someone else. Whichever side of that you are on, there's a need to address your own shadow nature in relationships and desires.

Rāhu pollutes the purity of Venus and the Moon, which, in their highest expression, represent an unconditional love. Rāhu often lowers the tone; through the thoughts you are having and the people you are attracting. Whatever your desire, including any particular fetish, it's never enough. But if you can acknowledge this, you may be able to enjoy the experience and recognise that there's more to life.

While you cannot deny the impulse of Rāhu in Rāhu daśā, you can take a step back while attempting to have your fill.

The primal brain is interested in keeping us safe, and in sex. So it should come as no surprise that sex and survival are intricately linked. Rāhu and Venus have a bond. Vedic myth tells about Śukracharya teaching the demons. Sex is the very reason you're here; but also, one of the reasons for the dwindling of your life force, spent all too easily without preservation of the essential juice that feeds your life.

From an Ayurvedic perspective, you are given a certain amount of 'battery juice' that you can spend quickly, or recharge as necessary. That juice is called *ojas*. Venus is the most refined planet, and ojas is the most refined and subtle essence of the physical body. When Rāhu gets involved with Venus, the refined is polluted. Rāhu's influence depletes ojas because the thing you crave leads to a loss of that very thing. A drug addict's need for the high leads to lows that they would never have known if not for their cravings. Rāhu cuts off the flow, as you try to keep more of it, strangling the life force and flow like a python strangles its prey.

Rāhu-Venus combinations represent the sudden urges you cannot control; the shadow side of your nature that is expressed in the most inappropriate ways; the parts you hide and project onto others whom you may label perverted. When the shadows combine with Venus, the sexual urge can show an obsession with sex or a complete denial; a manipulation of others for your own pleasure or being manipulated for someone else's pleasure or gain (gaslighting); to the most extreme expression: rape.

Both Rāhu-Venus and Rāhu-Moon have a profound impact on an individual's ability to control his or her sexual impulses. The main hormones involved in sex are dopamine and prolactin. Dopamine drives you to have sex over most other activities; but once you have a conventional orgasm, there is a drop in dopamine levels. It doesn't stay low, of course, as dopamine is highly addictive, and you're off again searching for the next high.

These highs can be very high, leading to risky sexual behaviour. The lows can be very low, making it difficult to get out of bed in the morning. After an exciting sexual encounter, or watching other novelty sexual encounters (porn), you may desperately seek new highs to raise your dopamine levels again. Dopamine drives ever more risk-taking and new sexual adventures - to get that high again.

If Venus is satisfaction, Rāhu is the magnifying lens that asks, 'Are you, really'? Rāhu says there's more, and more, and more to try! If that doesn't satisfy, try it this way. No? Let's try something else.

Sex is complex, of course, not just an itch you sometimes need to scratch. It's an emotionally and energetically fascinating act of will and submission, made all the more complex with the inclusion of the shadow of Rāhu.

Envy

Mercury and Saturn can represent envy, a feeling most of us are unlikely to admit to. Usually, we hide these feelings and allow them to come out in all kinds of distorted ways. Saturn can show a denial of something which leads to being envious of those who seem to have it. Mercury can show someone befriending a person they are envious of, with the purpose of getting something they have. They may ultimately sabotage the person's relationship or career, or whatever was the target of their envy.

Rāhu combined with Mercury or Saturn, either Rāhu in Gemini, Virgo, Capricorn, or Aquarius, or a Rāhu-Mercury or Rāhu-Saturn conjunction or time period, can bring up all kinds of issues around greed and envy. Yet you may not be able to acknowledge your feelings to even yourself. You may remain in the dark as to how to overcome this emotion. If you cannot acknowledge you are envious of someone who appears to be better off than you, you are unlikely to solve the issues in the best way possible; that is, by improving your own life so that you see yourself as on a par with them.

Rāhu combined with Mercury may show someone stealing from another, even simply by gossiping about them. This is stealing their reputation, damaging their image, so you don't have to feel envious of them. Rāhu combined with Saturn can show outright antagonism because of personal feelings of inadequacy.

The more evolved state of Rāhu in Mercury and Saturn's signs is certainly possible, which is about improving yourself, maybe even making others envious of you! Yet that will lead to its own problems eventually, as the pendulum of life swings in both directions. This tit-for-tat can be reflective of a Rāhu-Mercury and Rāhu-Saturn combination.

By becoming aware of the shadow at work when you are triggered by someone who seems more successful than you, don't forget it is your shadow that is reacting. It is a part of you that is feeling neglected that is the problem. The shadow part of you is successful and worthy of other people's envy, but you have long since denied it a voice. Seeing someone do all the things you wish you could serves as a reminder that you have neglected yourself. It has nothing to do with the other. In fact, you can thank someone the next time you feel envious of them. They are showing you something important about yourself, something that is holding you back from achieving all you want.

Attachment

Rāhu creates a false sense of self we get attached to. We protect neglected parts onto others to keep our false self functioning in society. In doing so, we get lost in the role we are playing, and in worldly pursuits. Rāhu is the driver of this illusion of self. Ketu, its opposite, cuts through these illusions so we can see the truth of who we really are. However, Ketu can often cut so much out of our lives that we are left feeling nothing but disillusioned. This is why Ketu is seen as a 'cruel planet' but also an awakener, removing all our illusions of a false self. This cutting away can ultimately lead to non-attachment, but only after we have struggled with letting go.

Rāhu attaches us to the world and is the very reason we have been born. We are here to experience life. But Ketu reminds us of where we have come from, in a spiritual sense. We come from nothing and return to nothing. But that nothing is full of everything. Ketu is the 'no-thing' that experiences the thing, the experiencer experiencing the experience. It is a vessel, an awareness of whatever is being experienced. When we forget that, we live in a state of delusion. Ketu is simply reminding us of this when we lose something or someone close. When someone close to us dies, we remember we come from somewhere else. And we remember we are all connected through the experience of death. Yet death itself is merely a gateway to a more profound sense of Self, beyond the physical self.

Ketu is always opposite Rāhu in the birth chart, as they are two points that line up on either side of the ecliptic to time the eclipses. This opposition reflects two sides of the same coin. While Ketu can remove the greed of Rāhu, the more extreme Rāhu becomes, the more extreme Ketu must become to counterbalance it. If you are obsessing about something because of Rāhu, and cannot let it go, Ketu's experience is most likely felt as utter annihilation. Everything seems to fall apart. If you are gripped by illusions of grandeur because of Rāhu, Ketu's extreme kicks in and shows your delusions by removing something. Yet you may only focus on the delusion, the attachment, and not focus on who is it that experiences such attachments.

Rāhu can show being out of touch with reality. Rāhu's unreality is reflected in attempting to 'be somebody'. Ketu can just as easily show you being deluded. The more disconnected you become in a Rāhu daśā, the further away from reality you drift, the more likely Ketu is felt as something negative. Yet there is also a sense that Ketu can be seen as disillusionment in a positive sense, a removal of all the many false selves.

This is one reason why Rāhu-Ketu sub-period is one of the more complex periods within the whole Rāhu daśā (more on this in *Nine Phases of Rāhu Daśā*). On the one hand, you are likely to still hunger for more life experience because of Rāhu. On the other, Ketu is likely to make you wish for something beyond this worldly realm altogether. The sense of disappointment from not having what you want, or having everything you wanted and still feeling empty, can lead to a sense of disillusionment and a connection to something far greater beyond.

Eclipses

Eclipses occur every six months, so they are not uncommon. They do not, however, impact everyone the same way. Usually, an eclipse will pass without much disruption, especially if someone is not in a Rāhu daśā or does not have a planet near the eclipse degree. If you are reading this, I imagine you are in a Rāhu daśā, or about to enter one, and could do with being more aware of the eclipse energy and what it brings about. But even if you are not, eclipses happen every year, so we could all do with understanding what they are about.

The primary thing an eclipse brings is exactly what Rāhu daśā brings; that is, change. If you are in a Rāhu daśā, you are primed for change more often, especially during the eclipses themselves. When an eclipse occurs, it simply shows more of a need for change at that time. If you also have planets near a particular eclipse degree, within about five degrees either side of where the eclipse takes place or in the opposite sign, change is an absolute certainty, and a must. Eclipses, just like Rāhu daśā, show you are evolving. Eclipses themselves can feel like major growth spurts, as your life takes a huge leap forward.

Even if you do not have planets near or opposite the eclipse degree, being in a Rāhu daśā means you are likely to feel the eclipses more intensely. Thus, you are likely to feel the need to make changes in the area of your life the eclipse is impacting by house position.

Eclipses show your evolution, one way or another. Usually, it's felt internally, as some internal shift of awareness takes place around the eclipse time. There may be a mental thrashing about that seems to occur, an intensity of feeling and of thoughts that gather speed and attention leading to the day of the eclipse. But the changes themselves may take place months before or after the actual eclipse date, when planets transit the eclipse degree.

During the eclipse itself, you may feel a sense of urgency to decide about something yet are unclear as to how to progress. You may think more about the pros and cons of a situation, and others might push you to decide, too.

It's important to recognise this time as one to temper the tendency to become mentally agitated and emotionally imbalanced. If you can temper these thoughts and feelings with something that steadies your mind on what is actually happening, it's probably going to help you make better decisions. Don't feel rushed into doing so, by anyone, around the eclipse time, at least. It's better to wait it out if possible and see how the chips fall. Everyone else is also feeling the intensity, to some degree or other, so they are not necessarily going to help you in your decision-making.

Take some time every six months about a week before and after the two-week period of the eclipses to quieten your life and free up your schedule as much as possible. While this may mean a whole month twice a year, you can be more present for the psychological changes happening for you before they become changes in the world around you. You can also look at the changes happening around you, as these are mirrors of what is going on inside you.

By being more mindful of these internal changes, recognising they are always internal first, you can then see how this leads to changes in your outer circumstances. Most people are likely to see changes taking place in their circumstances and tally that with the recent or upcoming eclipse but fail to recognise the inner change that was likely happening before this.

Whether a solar or lunar eclipse, and whether the Sun or Moon is conjunct Rāhu or Ketu, the transit of both Rāhu and Ketu, as well as the planets, show the timing of events, if there are to be any.

Solar Eclipses

A solar eclipse occurs whenever one of the lunar nodes, Rāhu or Ketu, conjoin the Sun or Moon. This can only occur during a New Moon. Solar eclipses are special New Moons for that reason. All New Moon phases are times to start again in some area of your life, with the solar eclipses being even more important periods of change and new beginnings.

New Moons are times of change each month, as the Moon reaches the Sun's degree and begins a new lunar cycle. The planetary alignments at the time of the New Moon express themselves in the month ahead. When Rāhu and Ketu line up within certain degrees of the Sun and Moon at this time, there is an eclipse. The alignments at the time have an impact, not just for the month ahead but for years.

A solar eclipse, whether total or partial, shows change for the part of your life highlighted by the eclipse degree. The house position and planets impacted show the areas ripe for change.

An eclipse can occur as soon as the Sun enters the sign in which Rāhu or Ketu are placed. All that's needed after that is the New or Full Moon phase, with the Moon joining or opposing the Sun's position.

Solar eclipses are more likely to bring bigger, longer-term changes to whatever areas are being impacted.

If the solar eclipse occurs before the lunar eclipse,

this means things are set in motion that reach a culmination around the Full Moon and lunar eclipse. When a solar eclipse occurs before a lunar, it is said to bring up more spiritual concerns, during the waxing phase of the Moon, leading to the Full Moon and lunar eclipse. Or to put it another way: the solar eclipse is more internal, as the Sun and Moon come together and reset something internally.

Lunar Eclipses

Lunar eclipses are generally more intense and immediate, as they stir the emotions in a more dramatic way. A lunar eclipse occurs when either node meets with the Sun, and the Moon opposes the Sun, i.e., a Full Moon. This can be a more external experience, a full experience, for better or worse. If there is something to enjoy, it can be very enjoyable indeed, perhaps too much so.

Emotions become heightened and can bring issues to a head, so you can resolve them. If a lunar eclipse occurs before a solar eclipse, there may be a more immediate concern that is brought up, which begins to wane during the waning phase of the Moon, leading to the reset point of the New Moon and solar eclipse.

It's important to keep things in perspective around the time of the lunar eclipse, and to keep the day of the eclipse itself free from as much distraction and decision-making as possible. If possible, keep the day for quiet contemplation. Avoid being around large crowds of people who are all feeling the intensity of the Full Moon and eclipse, as well. Full Moons are already quite intense emotionally. Eclipsed Moons are even more so. This could be intensely good, of course, but even then there may be a tendency to overindulge.

Anytime the Moon is more extreme, either New or Full, and especially eclipsed, there is a tendency for the mind to go to extremes. Allow for this by creating a safe space where you can manage the energy. Eventually, the intensity subsides, and you can make your next move with a cool head.

It is at the times of the eclipses that you may feel a sense of urgency to do something, or to decide about something pressing. Yet the advice is usually to hold off on making any decisions about important things, to allow the disturbed energy to settle before making your mind up. Too many things are in flux during the eclipses themselves for you to be able to see the situation clearly. Until the shadows pass, you may not see the full picture, even if you have some profound insights about something. The issue with the eclipses, and the nodes in general, is that, no matter how much insight you experience, there's always the potential for a distortion.

Imagine you are looking at something with a magnifying glass. Rahu can magnify whatever it looks at, which allows you to see deeper into the issue. But a magnifying glass also distorts the light. Once you remove it, you can take those new perspectives with you as you take a step back and reassess the situation.

Myth of Rāhu & Ketu

The Hindu myth *Samudra Manthan* tells the story of Svarbhānu, the demon who distracted the gods to drink of the immortal nectar. Viṣṇu, the preserver of the universe, saw this deceit and cut the demon's head off, thus creating Rāhu, the head, and Ketu, the headless body. Yet the demon had already consumed the immortal nectar and thus became immortal, forever chasing the Sun and Moon. Twice a year, they overshadow the luminaries, during the eclipses.

This myth tells us a little about our own shadow nature, our hunger for something. We will do whatever it takes to get it, usually presenting ourselves as something we are not. Rāhu shows what we want, the personas and masks we wear to get what we want, while Ketu shows what we may reject on some level, having had our fill.

In the Samudra Manthan, the 'churning of the oceans of milk' took place before the elixir appeared and was shared between the gods. The snake Vasuki was used to churn the oceans of milk, with the gods on one side and the demons on the other. The churning revealed many treasures and poisons. This is analogous of our own gods and demons, the good and bad thoughts that thrash about in our heads, weighing up the pros and cons of a situation. This thrashing about becomes more intense in Rāhu daśā, and especially during the eclipses.

The treasures and poisons of the mind are further enhanced in Rāhu daśā. The churning of the oceans of milk not only produced poisons; it also produced its cure. This story tells about our own ability to overcome our blind spots, a virus of the mind.

Rāhu represents viruses of the body as well. This great churning of the oceans is playing out in a modern context in quite literal ways. In the push for a treatment for a virus in the early 2020s, it's as if the gods and demons were thrashing about looking for the elixir. The global pandemic that began in 2020 is pointing to something far greater than our physical health. It is reminding us of our connection to each other. Death unifies us all. Pandemics remind us to connect with that which is beyond things that separate us. Our shared fears allow us to think on a larger scale and connect with one another and our shared pain, a unity arising from a sense of separation. While there is the very real pain of people dying and leaving behind loved ones, there is the illusion that we are separate beings to begin with.

Back at the royal banquet, the demigod Svarbhānu wanted the immortal nectar that was being distributed to the gods, so he disguised himself as a beautiful woman, Mohinī, to sneak his way in-between the Sun and Moon, to obtain it for himself. That alone will tell you a lot about the nature of Rāhu, the head of the demon, where all our desires lie. It tells us of our deceit in getting what we want and the lengths we go to disguise ourselves in doing so. We take on the role of imposter when we have an ambition and must 'fake it til we make it'.

Just as a drop of the immortal nectar was taken by Svarbhānu, Viṣṇu saw this deceit and threw his discus at the demon, cutting off his head, the head becoming Rāhu, and the body, Ketu. Yet the demon had become immortal, the head severed from the body. This tells us of the price we must pay for our ambition to get something. Whatever you get during your Rāhu daśā, whatever success you achieve, there is always a price to pay. And even then, you feel like an imposter when you get it. This is never more apparent then when you gain a position for which you are not ready. You may have even lied about your abilities to get it. When you find yourself in a position of power, you may feel like an imposter, just like Svarbhānu. You may even deceive others around you for some time, but eventually you are found out. You must trip up. It's all part of the script.

You may work in the background, scheming your next move, hidden from others who you think will take it from you. You may overshadow others or even take credit for the work they do.

Rāhu and Ketu are always working away in the background, outside your conscious awareness, or others' awareness. Rāhu is said to represent ultraviolet on the colour spectrum, and Ketu, infrared. These are outside the range visible to the naked eye. It's only when you are in a Rāhu or Ketu period, and/or during an eclipse, that they come into your conscious awareness. Whatever you were hiding in the areas the eclipse occurs is brought to light. Yet other things are hidden behind the shadows, to be revealed some other time.

Viruses are a good example of how Rāhu operates. Rāhu can be seen as a mental virus, faulty perspectives that infect your mind. Viruses hijack cells, just like Svarbhānu hijacked the party to grab the immortal nectar for himself. They feed off cells to stay alive, although they are not alive themselves. This is reflected in the birth chart by Rāhu or Ketu being unable to operate without a host planet. The planets that rule the signs they are in show how they express themselves. This relationship is a two-way street. The planets ruling the signs they are in function as hosts, keeping them alive. Viruses may cause illness, but they also keep the host alive.

Just as Rāhu had his head cut off, but became

immortal, you too experience this in Rāhu daśā. You must have your head cut off, to lose yourself to your desire for something. Eventually, you become immune to Rāhu. In other words, you learn to respond to life's ups and downs with more discernment, from a place of stillness. Instead of wishing to 'be somebody', you settle down and simply be.

You make peace with the parts you reject; you eventually make peace with all that is, the 'good' and 'bad', in yourself and in others. You realise you are the other.

Withdrawing your shadow projections, you play your part in becoming whole.

Polarizing Signs

Each sign of the zodiac is polarized, in a way. Every sign has its opposite, which shows an extreme on the other end of a spectrum. Aries, for example, is opposite Libra, in that selfish pursuits are opposite to a willingness to compromise. Taurus is opposite Scorpio, in that feelings of stability are opposite feelings of uncertainty.

Rāhu and Ketu in their opposite signs exaggerate the split, as if the head is separated from the body. The signs in which Rāhu and Ketu are placed, either natally or by transit, display more extremes. Rāhu can show obsessions and compulsions, while Ketu can show neglect and impulsions. Rāhu wishes to devour whatever it touches, while Ketu shows where you have had your fill. Ketu is your default setting, in a way. It can show where you reap the rewards or lament your mistakes, depending.

Aries-Libra

We experience all the signs in different areas of our life. Although, generally, Aries and Libra represent the self and the other, someone with Cancer ascendant would have Aries in the 10th house of work and may be more selfish at work, but more compromising in their personal lives (Libra in the 4th house). They must learn to achieve a work/life balance. This becomes more polarized when Rāhu, and its polar opposite node, Ketu, are placed in these signs.

Their opposing forces bring out these signs' shadow natures more so, generally overemphasizing one (Rāhu) and neglecting the other (Ketu). Yet by overemphasizing and exaggerating one, both become distorted. Exaggerating one, while neglecting or even rejecting the other, distorts both of them. Fearing and neglecting something usually makes it something bigger and scarier in our minds than it may actually be in reality. Overly focusing on something distorts the reality of the situation.

Whatever signs Rāhu and Ketu are in, it can swing wildly, yet unconsciously, from one extreme to the other. You may not be aware of it, but someone with Rāhu in Aries and Ketu in Libra may swing between radical independence and authenticity, to being overly accommodating and compromising. If someone has these signs in the 1st and 7th houses, this becomes even more extreme, as their interpersonal relations swing from being fiercely independent and jumping into relationship after relationship to try to find this balance.

Taurus-Scorpio

Rāhu-Ketu in Taurus-Scorpio exaggerates financial and family matters. This can show up in all kinds of ways, but the core issue is the same. Rāhu in either Taurus or Scorpio is more extreme, as Rāhu is said to be exalted in Taurus and debilitated in Scorpio. This means Rāhu behaves in more extreme ways. Whether extremely 'good' or 'bad', either can flip to the opposite extreme.

Rāhu in Taurus can be so good, in that you may experience many comforts and luxuries in life, but you may not ever feel you have enough. The greed of Rāhu can eventually lead to losses. An example of this is someone taking on one financial risk too many and losing it all. A business person, no matter how successful, may feel they need yet another company and buy out one that eventually sinks them. Rāhu in Taurus places Ketu in Scorpio, highlighting the split between looking at the surface of things for certainty (Taurus), while neglecting the potential for loss and uncertainty (Ketu in Scorpio).

Rāhu in Scorpio may show the opposite extreme, of only looking at problems and perhaps not having enough security and stability as a result. There may be a constant vigilance to threat that the person may not ever take risks that would actually lead to more success, and the stability they need. In this case, Ketu in Taurus would highlight the neglect of even the basics in life, such as family support, good nutrition, and community involvement. If someone is dwelling on the depths in Scorpio, no matter how insightful this is, they may not give themselves the support they need to continue diving deep.

Gemini-Sagittarius

Rāhu-Ketu in Gemini-Sagittarius can show a split between opinions and learning from others. Some Indian astrologers postulate that Rāhu is exalted in Gemini. Its association with Mercury, which it is seen as 'friendly to', can certainly show more strength for Rāhu. Yet strong isn't always a good thing, as viewed in Rāhu's recent transit in Gemini during a global pandemic of 2020.

Rāhu exaggerates and distorts. In Gemini, this means distorting communications. Rāhu in Gemini may show a skewed opinion that has no basis in truth (Ketu in Sagittarius). Although it can show many great ideas and insightful opinions, it can just as easily show a lack of truth. As always, Rāhu tends to show all or nothing, swinging wildly from one to the other. Someone may have a lot of opinions with Rāhu in

Gemini, and many great things to say, but lack faith. Gemini flips things over in the mind, with Rāhu further challenging them to stay level-headed. Eventually, the mind can become overwhelmed with all the seeming contradictions, with no firm footing in something beyond as they attempt to work it out intellectually.

Conversely, Rāhu in Sagittarius may challenge because of an overemphasis on faith. It may show a lack of personal opinion in favour of what is being taught. If the onus is placed on a teacher or teaching with little or no regard for their own experience, their own ability to work it out for themselves, they may be just as lost. If something doesn't resonate with you, no matter how well-presented by someone else, if it's not true for you, how true is it? Rāhu in Sagittarius can show being overly focused on traditions, but also being confused because of having too many people saying different things. An example of this is someone who doesn't trust their own intuition, seeking out advice from many different sources. The more sources they find, the less sure they are of themselves. Seeking advice itself is, in a way, telling yourself you don't trust your instincts. If you need someone else to tell you what to do, you are likely neglecting what you know to be true. Yet you could also take advice and apply it, to see if it's true-for you. This is a more evolved state of the nodes in these signs. Yet you must be aware of the tendency for Ketu in Gemini to reflect a lack of rationality and ability in discriminating fact from fiction. As Rāhu in Sagittarius exaggerates and distorts knowledge, Ketu in Gemini takes it and runs with it, without thinking things through.

Cancer-Capricorn

Rāhu-Ketu in Cancer-Capricorn can show a split between home and work, private and public life. Rāhu in Cancer exaggerates and distorts emotional bonds and attachments. This can show someone manipulating close family bonds and relationships, leading to co-dependency.

Rāhu exaggerates Cancer's tendency to bond in more extreme ways. Yet there may be a fear of dealing with their own emotional issues when someone focuses on others. Or there may be a fear of dealing with the world 'out there' (Ketu in Capricorn), as someone puts all their focus and attention on home life and safety. Rāhu in Cancer can show an intense need for safety and security, which sends a signal that one is unsafe. The more someone locks up the house, each turn of the key or bolting of the homestead can actually send a signal of threat. No matter how much someone is locked up inside, whether literally or figurately, there is an avoidance of the 'big bad world' out there.

Rāhu in Capricorn can show the other extreme of only focusing on the world and worldly success, to the detriment of home life and personal happiness (Ketu in Cancer). The person may neglect their house and home in favour of being at work. The work-life balance is thrown off and may swing wildly from one extreme to another. Someone may spend too much time at work and not enough at home, but then exhaust themselves in the search for promotion, leaving them feeling a sense of lack when they get it. If they're not addressing home life and their private self, the overemphasis on the public self can simply reinforce a sense of lack of emotional stability, which they actually need to become successful. As the saying goes, "The tree can only grow as tall as the roots are deep."

Leo-Aquarius

Rāhu-Ketu in Leo-Aquarius can show a split between children, friends, creative self-expression, and group think-tanks. Whether someone has children, or just friends, the issues are about what is dear to the person versus what others have to say about it.

Rāhu in Leo exaggerates and distorts personal choice and preference over others' needs. It can show someone having a strong need to find themselves in their children, or creative self-expression, their personal power and freedom to choose what they want, that they neglect what even society thinks about it (Ketu in Aquarius). This actually comes from a lack of a sense of self (Rāhu in Leo), which may play out in an inability to connect to groups at large. To connect with others, in a community, or in society, you must know yourself.

Yet Rāhu in Leo shows an exaggerated sense of self, which is untrue. This is likely to be starkly felt by others who come into contact with someone with Rāhu in Leo.

Rāhu in Aquarius exaggerates and distorts the need to connect with groups at large, to form new ideas and progress within society, that the person may completely neglect their own self (Ketu in Leo) in favour of what others think. This can block progress, ultimately.

Someone tinkering in a lab or working on a new idea within a network may not focus enough on what it is that fuels them personally. Yet when they do, their individual spark can lead to greater innovations within the group context. Sitting at a boardroom meeting requires this kind of balancing act. You must bring your unique ideas and personality, but you must be able to take feedback and bounce your ideas off the group. Someone with Rāhu-Ketu in Leo-Aquarius may find this balancing act more of a challenge, but the more the challenge, the greater the rewards.

Virgo-Pisces

Rāhu-Ketu in Virgo-Pisces can show a split between daily routines and getting away, between working out problems and letting them go. These, like all Rāhu-Ketu dynamics, are issues that may take a lifetime to resolve.

Rāhu in Virgo exaggerates and distorts daily life and its inherent problems, to the point where the person may not be able to switch off and recharge completely (Ketu in Pisces). On the other hand, this may also show someone completely shutting down and not dealing with problems, tuning out with some substance or activity that allows them to dissolve into the great unknown. Rāhu in Virgo is seen as a powerful placement according to some Indian astrologers, as it is friendly to Mercury and in an earth sign. This can stabilize Rāhu. Yet Rāhu's association with Mercury can still overstimulate the mind. It shows someone trying to work out every little detail and form some order out of chaos. While the pursuit is noble, the issue is becoming so bogged down in details that you never swich off the mind.

Rāhu in Pisces, on the other end of the spectrum, may show someone focusing solely on switching off, not dealing with anything in a practical way. They may use substances to aid in this, or even spiritual practices, just so they can avoid dealing with their problems (Ketu in Virgo). The term "spiritual bypassing" was coined by psychologist John Welwood, which describes Rāhu-Ketu in Pisces-Virgo very well. Yet Rāhu in Pisces could also elevate a person to greater heights of perception, so much so that they see solutions to everyday problems in ways someone overly focusing on them cannot.

Rāhu-Ketu in all the signs brings some distortion in the areas of the life impacted, based on their house positions in your birth chart (see chapter on *Rāhu in Each Sign and House*).

Masculine & Feminine Signs

Each sign is either more masculine or feminine. The masculine signs are opposite each other, as are the feminine signs. Rāhu and Ketu exaggerate and distort masculine and feminine traits wherever they are. Aries and Libra are masculine signs. Rāhu in Aries and Ketu in Libra is likely to show some distortion around masculine themes, either an overemphasis on masculinity, or a lack of its positive qualities and shadow projections. The same is true for Gemini-Sagittarius and Leo-Aquarius.

Psychiatrist Carl Jung referred to these as the animus (masculine), and anima (feminine). A man is more likely to repress his feminine qualities and project it onto a woman he gets involved with, while a woman represses her masculine qualities and projects them onto the man. While this may seem as if we are moving beyond stereotypical masculine and feminine roles in society, it's actually distorting these more because of our current insistence on denying the distinct masculine and feminine traits we all have. They then become shadow material for the lunar nodes. We project more toxic masculinity and femininity onto others who more obviously display these.

As Rāhu and Ketu are always opposite, and as they are always either in masculine or feminine signs, it's important to acknowledge our masculine and feminine traits in all its many ways. We all have masculine and feminine traits, although we have one more than the other and usually conform to gender norms. When Rāhu daśā begins, see if these norms are challenged in some way.

A simpler way of observing this is to see if Rāhu and Ketu are in masculine or feminine signs in your birth chart. You can also see how many planets you have in masculine and feminine signs, adding up your totals to get an overall picture of whether you are more masculine or feminine. You can also include your ascendant, as this says a lot about how you approach life.

The masculine signs are Aries, Gemini, Leo, Libra, Sagittarius and Aquarius. The feminine signs are Taurus, Cancer, Virgo, Scorpio, Capricorn, and Pisces. Although this is seen as politically incorrect in our current social climate, reflecting how it strengthens the shadow aspects of masculinity and femininity, this isn't the same as whether you are a man or a woman. Men can be more feminine and women more masculine. Someone who has more planets in feminine signs may have a masculine rising sign like Aries. Although they may do things in a masculine, maybe a more forceful way, they may be more feminine overall. Chart interpretation is a more nuanced dynamic than I am portraying here, of course.

The masculine and feminine have different expressions according to how evolved they are. The Sun represents the masculine principle in its most evolved state, as pure presence, but only if the Sun is unobstructed and strongly placed. Any affliction of the Sun distorts the masculine impulse. Someone with a weak Sun in Libra, for example, without any mitigating factors, may have an issue with expressing their masculinity. This may lead to either not expressing it very much, or at all, or overcompensating for a lack and becoming pushy. A man is more likely to overcompensate for this to prove he's a man. If Rāhu were involved with the Sun, this may become even more distorted. The father relationship may be strained or imbalanced in some way. There may be a great hunger to express masculinity in the form of success and achievement. This is telling of the block of Rāhu and the lack the person experienced early on.

The Moon represents the feminine principle. In its most evolved state, it is unconditional love. This may be seen in someone with a strong and unafflicted Moon. Any affliction to the Moon can show a distortion of the feminine principle of intuitive care and natural instinct. This is distinct from the Sun's role as enforcer, the externalizing force of the more internal Moon qualities. If Rāhu is with the Moon, this may become even more distorted (see chapter on *Rāhu Conjoined Planets*).

Rāhu-Moon connections may block someone's ability to express the feminine in its most evolved state of unconditional love, potentially leading to a lack of care of oneself and others. Or opposite extremes may be expressed, i.e., being overly focused on how one feels, or being hypersensitive to others' feelings.

Once the nodes are involved, the more evolved states of the masculine and feminine can be projected onto a partner of a different sex. Anyone, of any gender, can experience this. It's more important to recognise when you are extreme in one way or the other. If you are extremely masculine, e.g. Mars in Aries ascendant, you may project the feminine onto a partner who will express your repressed feminine qualities. If Rāhu were also involved with Mars, this can further exaggerate and distort the masculine impulse. You may be overly brutish or project this onto others whom you label so.

Relationships that are set up in this extreme way rarely run smoothly. They are too polarized. There may be an extreme attraction, but unless and until you can incorporate and assimilate your repressed masculine or feminine, you are likely to swing wildly in and out of relationships until you find more balance. The more balanced and integrated your masculine and feminine qualities are, the more balanced your relationships will be.

This is never more the case than when Rāhu and Ketu are placed in the 1st and 7th house of the horoscope. When someone has this combination, their life lesson is about finding an appropriate balance between themselves and others. They may feel drawn into relationship after relationship (Rāhu in 7th), not realizing they are sabotaging it so they can continue the chase. At the same time, they may not be willing to look at their repressed masculine or feminine and continue to experience the other as an extreme. The pendulum must swing back in the other direction eventually. If Rāhu were in the 7th, Ketu must be in the 1st, showing a loss of a sense of self that eventually sabotages relationships if one cannot hold space for the other. The other extreme expression of this is overthinking relationships, even obsessing about others, to the point where they may neglect themselves. And yet, their obsession to be in a relationship is what prevents them from forming healthy ones.

With Rāhu in the 1st and Ketu in the 7th, the focus is on the self, often to the exclusion of the other. Yet this may unconsciously swing to the opposite extreme, as and when someone overly focuses on relationships to express themselves more. They are more likely to sabotage the relationship if their freedom is threatened, as the other is merely an opportunity to connect with different parts of themselves. Rāhu in the 1st can show not having a strong sense of self, which eventually leads to narcissistic behaviours. Recognising these behaviors as a way to reconnect with themselves will help heal the divisions and form healthier relationships.

If either of these dynamics, Rāhu in the 1st or 7th, occurs in masculine signs, toxic masculinity may be experienced, whether with a man or woman. This can take the form of competitiveness in the relationship. If this occurs in feminine signs, toxic femininity may take the form of emotional manipulations.

Rāhu and Ketu do not only cause imbalances in relationships though, as all areas of life are in relationship to their opposite, i.e., all signs have an opposite. Wherever Rāhu and Ketu are placed, they represent areas of life that usually experience a more extreme split that eventually must be integrated and healed.

Rāhu in Each Sign & House

Your experience of Rāhu daśā will be coloured by its house and sign position in your birth chart. Also, the house position of Aquarius, the sign Rāhu rules, shows what Rāhu represents for you. Rāhu's house position shows your blind spot, where your intense desire is also likely blocked from getting what you want – but also how to get it. The sign position of Rāhu shows how well you deal with it. The planet that rules the sign in question, its position and strength, will also have an impact on how you manage it.

Rāhu is a shadow. It needs a planet to express itself through. Much like a virus needs a cell to 'stay alive', Rāhu needs a host, becoming a virus in your mind. The degree to which you can handle its extremes depends on its strength and the strength of the planet that rules the sign it is in.

According to *Brihat Parasara Hora Sastra* (Sharma 2006), Rāhu is exalted in Taurus and debilitated in Scorpio. Taurus tends to stabilise Rāhu in the down-to-earth realms of Taurus, leading to the potential for many enjoyable experiences. Yet this has its own pitfalls. Overindulging the senses creates problems eventually. On the other hand, the senses are the most stabilizing thing to focus on if the mind has wandered in Rāhu daśā.

Rāhu in Taurus may be enjoyable, but it may also show psychological blocks, even when there is plenty of things to enjoy. Rāhu in Taurus is like someone having a million in the bank and not being able to enjoy it because of worrying about it running out. Eventually, it may indeed run out. Rāhu in Taurus can show extreme highs and lows financially. Rāhu is insatiable, a part of your being that has not tasted what it longs for in this life. No amount of that thing is likely to satiate your hunger. It may take time for someone to experience problems of overindulgence, but they eventually show up. Starvation, another extreme expression of Rāhu in the 2nd house, of which Taurus is indicative of, may be obvious from the get-go. Starvation, or not getting the things in life you want, shows up right away. Greed takes its time to show up as a problem. Both extremes leave you without or feeling like you are.

Rāhu in Scorpio is a challenge no matter, exaggerating and distorting all kinds of problems in one's mind. Rāhu in Scorpio may show someone dwelling on life's uncertainties, forgoing basic comforts (Taurus), or failing to recognise them as an important part of life as they go through one transformative process after another. Each planets' rulership and strength will show how well you manage the affairs of the sign and house Rāhu is in. For simplicity, you can take a sign as a house, and a house as a sign.

Here is a list of each sign and the planet or planets that are said to 'rule it'. This means each planet represents the sign and area of life the sign is placed by house position. Simply, each sign is a house or place in your life through which you experience each planet.

Sign	Ruler(s)
Aries	Mars
Taurus	Venus
Gemini	Mercury
Cancer	Moon
Leo	Sun
Virgo	Mercury
Libra	Venus
Scorpio	Mars and Ketu
Sagittarius	Jupiter
Capricorn	Saturn
Aquarius	Saturn and Rāhu
Pisces	Jupiter

The strength of each planet shows how you experience each house, each place the planet rules in your life. The following list shows the more extreme strengths and weaknesses of each planet. This is a lot more nuanced than presented here, as there are many other factors to determine strength, and many mitigating factors for each. If you know the sidereal positions of the planets in your birth chart, you can add this to Rāhu's position in whatever sign by looking at the ruler of this sign and its strength. Is the planet moving towards or away from its exaltation? Is it placed in its own sign? See the list of *Signs* and their *Rulers*.

The strength of the planet that rules the sign Rāhu is in will show if you express Rāhu's more evolved states. If the planet that rules the sign Rāhu is in move towards its degree of exaltation, it has greater strength. If it's moving towards its degree of debilitation, it is weaker, although this is usually mitigated by other factors in the birth chart.

Planet	Exaltation	Debilitation
Sun	Aries 10°	Libra 10°
Moon	Taurus 3°	Scorpio 3°
Mars	Capricorn 28°	Cancer 28°
Mercury	Virgo 15°	Pisces 15°
Jupiter	Cancer 5°	Capricorn 5°
Venus	Pisces 27°	Virgo 27°
Saturn	Libra 20°	Aries 20°

Aries & 1st House

Rāhu in Aries or the 1st house can exaggerate one's sense of self. Yet it could just as easily show a lack of confidence in who you are and what you are doing. Narcissism is just that, it seems: a disconnection from oneself which leads to an exaggerated sense of self. It's the lack that leads to the overcompensation. No one is fooled by brutish bravado. Yet you may indeed have to start there to try to find the courage to overcome your shortcomings.

The shadow side of Aries and Mars is aggression because of a lack of strength. Someone who feels strong has no need to assert themselves in such extreme ways. The shadow of Aries can also show a lack of drive, a lack of libido, a dampening down of what seems hard to control. Energy might come in spurts, actions impulsive, even reckless, especially in youth. As someone with this combination gets older, they may be able to focus it more and restrain themselves. But therein lies a problem. If you overdo that impulse, there's no outlet for Rāhu to express its raw energy and emotion through high octane activities. A balance may be reached by knowing when to move, to act, and when to be still, to sit back and allow things to happen, not needing to prove anything to anyone.

Mars' strength and placement reflects how well you manage yours and others' expectations of yourself. You may rally everything you have at projecting yourself into the world around you or slip back into obscurity if you feel threatened. It may swing wildly from one extreme to the other.

Rāhu in the 1st house or Aries may show up in you asking too much of yourself, precisely because you don't feel as if you are enough just for who you are. This highlights the extreme ends of Rāhu. It is all or nothing. You may feel like you are more than you are, yet this may hide your inadequacies. You may try even harder to impress others. Or you may focus so much on what you are not, attempting to be more, that you may end up with Rāhu's more extreme expression of narcissism. We're all narcissistic in some form and to some degree, but Rāhu in the 1st or Aries can further exaggerate this tendency.

The main issue is not feeling you are enough, as if you have to prove something. But no matter how much you achieve, it will never fill the void. The challenge is to recognise that you are indeed enough and that you have nothing to prove to yourself or anyone else.

Trying to prove yourself is itself reflective of you not feeling you are enough, just as you are. Simply being alive should be enough proof that the universe is conspiring to keep you here. But you may not see it that way. If you have Rāhu in this position you may try hard to 'be somebody' that you disconnect from life itself, from simply being alive. Ambition is the most disconnecting experience. You may project an ideal self into an imagined future.

Mars' position and strength will say a lot about how you handle Rāhu in Aries. If powerful and well-positioned, Rāhu can be channelled courageously and advantageously. On the other hand, Mars' extremes of exaltation or debilitation, in Capricorn or Cancer, can show up as extremes in behaviour that may require more temperance.

A weak Mars in Cancer may show up as a lack of motivation, which Rāhu in Aries will only further exaggerate. This may be through some sort of overcompensation or acts of rebellion, or by not trying at all. You may become a doormat or a tyrant, depending.

A strong Mars in Capricorn may show up as a powerful sense of self and selfish needs, which may need to be tempered when dealing with others' needs. Otherwise, you may rub others up the wrong way. You may enjoy the challenge, of course, as the strength of Mars reflects a personal need to excel in whatever you do. To excel means to step on others' toes at times. To get ahead means you may make an enemy or two.

Whatever the strength of Mars in your chart, it's important to recognise where this need to prove yourself is coming from and if you could do with easing up on the acceleration at times. Getting a balance right between over- or under-doing it will be your lesson, not needing to prove yourself to anyone, least of all yourself.

Taurus & 2nd House

Rāhu in Taurus or the 2nd house can exaggerate finances, food, family dynamics, values, vision (both actual vision and an inner vision), and speech. As usual, Rāhu can show up in extremes. You may have a lot of wealth, but then go bankrupt. You may speak excessively or not at all. You may swing from one extreme to the other. If you say too much, you're likely to have to be quiet for some time. You may eat a very strict diet at times, and then overindulge. If you haven't been diagnosed with an eating disorder, you may at least identify with disordered eating habits. You may feel disconnected from your family or community, building your own. Yet you may feel like the 'black sheep', within your family of origin or community, if indeed you involve yourself with a community at all.

You may feel you have followed your family's values to the point where you don't know what you personally value apart from them, and then overcompensate by going it alone to try to figure out what's more important to you. You may wish to increase your own value by earning in ways that are not seen as ethical by others, without any help from others. Or you may simply earn by becoming ruthless. You may be quite resourceful, but only because you have to be. You may not feel like you ever have enough, even if you have plenty. Whether you do or not, whatever amount you have in the bank or in your food cupboard, it may not feel like enough. In that case, it doesn't matter if you are reasonably well off or a billionaire.

The core issue is not feeling you are worthy. Your family may not have instilled that in you through no fault of their own. You may not have been fed well, for example. Good food, shelter, and the basics in life, may have been denied you in some way. You may overcompensate by earning a great deal. You may hold onto your wealth so tightly that you end up stopping the flow. You may stranglehold all your resources, becoming miserly, which can lead to a lack of resources eventually. Even if you maintain a large bank balance, miserliness itself is a state of lack.

You must learn to value yourself and see that you are worthy, whatever you have, that you are deserving. While your family of origin may not have made you feel worthy, either because they did not look after your basic needs or didn't do so in a way that felt right to you, the lesson here is how to look after yourself now, without overcompensating. If you take this to extremes with Rāhu in Taurus or the 2nd house, you may try to fill a void with things that simply don't make you feel full. This can literally be the case with overindulging with your diet. Someone may become obsessive about healthy eating, after having eaten a poor diet in earlier years, or vice versa. If you are too focused on healthy eating you may end up with an eating disorder such as orthorexia, where an initial need to eat healthy may lead to an unhealthy balance. This impulse may come from an initial lack of proper nutrition early in life, either because of a lack of finances or simply a lack of proper knowledge about nutrition. Usually, Rāhu in Taurus or the 2nd house shows a lack of something in the diet, but more often than not it is because of some extreme dieting or fad diet. If there are any extremes in any way, there must be something lacking in another way. So, best to avoid extreme diets with Rāhu in Taurus or the 2nd house, and to stick with a varied diet. Be mindful of eating foods that are contaminated also.

Vision is another important component of the 2nd house and Taurus. Again, Rāhu can show up as extremes. You may have great insights but lack a clear vision of how to move forward. You may miss something right in front of you by obsessing about seeing deeply into something.

Venus' strength and position will show how much you can enjoy Rāhu in Taurus, and which particular focus of the 2nd house is more important. Look to the house position of Venus and the 2nd house ruling planet. All the basics of food, shelter, family and wealth, are all important, but Rāhu can obscure your view and favour one over the other. Venus in the 7th house of relationships coupled with Rāhu in Taurus or the 2nd house may reflect a need for more notches on your bedpost, for example. There may be a need to have more sexual indulgences and relationships to fill the void of Rāhu. Or it may show an oral fixation in sex. No matter how much you try to satisfy the itch, wherever the itch is felt, another one comes along for your attention.

Venus in a weak position in Virgo may show up as not ever feeling happy with whatever is showing up in your experience. You may be a perfectionist who is never fulfilled. Either you don't get what or who you want, or you don't get it the way you want it.

Venus in a strong position in Pisces may express an ideal situation or idealised love that no one person can satisfy. You may instead attempt to fill the void through a love for humanity, either through religious or spiritual outlets, or through some sort of service-orientated roles. Or you may find expression in some form of creative outlet.

Whatever the state and strength of Venus, Rāhu in Taurus or the 2nd house can express a longing for a stability that Rāhu does not always provide. Instead, Rāhu prefers excitement and change. This can be facilitated through transforming your relationship to people and things, so you can see that satisfying your worldly desires ultimately takes you beyond worldly dissatisfaction.

Gemini & 3rd House

Rāhu in Gemini or the 3rd house, the sign and house of communications, can express itself as a lot of opinions. But who are you trying to convince? Rāhu can show a lack of confidence in communication, which you may overcompensate for. You may, at times, forcefully express yourself, while, at others, lack clarity or appropriate communications skills, especially with with the most important elements of good communication, i.e., listening. You may not listen to anyone else's opinion or be overly sensitive to them if you feel you've overstepped the mark. As usual, Rāhu tends to swing from one extreme to another.

You may be so focused on what you have to say that you neglect to think about anyone else. This can lead to all kinds of selfish behaviour. Your interactions with others may be extreme. You may have intense interactions for some time and then nothing. You may find ways to work around this, other ways of expressing yourself and your needs while staying open to what others have to say. You may find manipulative ways to get what you want, beyond shouting for it. You may 'fight dirty'. You may be jealous of what others have but may not show it. Instead, you may use all kinds of tactics to get what others have.

Relationships with siblings and neighbours growing up would have had a big impact on your communications skills, as well as how you get what you want. These relationships may continue to challenge you to be clear about it, without overdoing it.

Rāhu in Gemini and the 3rd house can express the baser instincts such as gossiping about others. You may be envious about what another has and want it for yourself. If you cannot get it, you may spoil it for them.

Mercury's strength and position will show how well you manage all this, how you communicate whatever it is you want. This will also show how you engage with your libido, as Gemini represents sex. You may swing (pardon the pun!) wildly between being promiscuous and chaste. Rāhu here can show both a fear and fascination of the darker side of sex. You may direct your libido into other pursuits and skills. While you may not have intercourse with anyone, you may flirt a lot to overcome any sexual inadequacies.

Mercury's weakness in Pisces can show a mind that is confused about what it wants in the first place. You may be overwhelmed by choice and debate, not being able to discriminate fact from fiction. Indeed, Rāhu may be fictitious, but its goal is to find ultimate truth. Mercury in Pisces cannot deal with all the potentials and possibilities. Your mind may not be able to cope. Yet this may bring out your more creative side, one you would not have had access to otherwise.

Mercury's strength in Virgo can show an ability to discriminate fact from fiction, despite Rāhu's tendency to confuse. You may, at least, develop a better understanding and rationality, despite Rāhu's irrationality. You may become hyper-rational, which is itself a kind of irrationality. An exalted Mercury may be good for managing your life, but you may attempt to micro-manage and overdo it. Rāhu knows no boundaries. It can overdo anything, even if the impulse was correct in the first instance.

Whatever Mercury's strength, Rāhu in Gemini or the 3rd house shows how well you get what you want, including how well you communicate this to others.

Cancer & 4th House

Rāhu in Cancer or the 4th house shows an intense need for happiness and safety, a chase for which can actually sabotage your peace of mind. You may not realise it, but the pursuit of happiness is itself one way to guarantee you are not happy (see the chapter, *The Pursuit of Happiness*). By constantly seeking ways to be happy, you are telling yourself, albeit subconsciously, that you are not where you want to be.

You may seek out all the ways you can to be happy. You may move house a lot or change the country you live in, seeking that elusive sense of external happiness, without realising happiness is fleeting, that there is an inner joy you can have no matter the outer circumstances. In your attempt to stabilise something that is fleeting, you may cause more problems than you solve. If you cannot let things be as they are, to be happy whatever is, you may constantly struggle to find the setting you think will fill the void. The more you can see this, the more joyful you can be whatever the outer circumstances.

Your relationship with your mother and homelife will form much of these dynamics early on. Rāhu tends to block certain relationships from running smoothly.

In doing so, you can learn to cultivate self-care and protection from within.

The Moon's strength and position will show how you go about attaching yourself to healthy pursuits and relationships. A debilitated Moon in Scorpio may show an unhealthy fascination with the macabre. You may think up the worst-case scenario to prepare yourself mentally and emotionally for something that is unlikely to ever happen. In doing so, you simply subject your mind to negative thinking. Although you may be more prepared if such a catastrophy were ever to occur, you may just as easily weaken yourself and are unable to react appropriately when another challenging situation arises. But at least you can tell yourself "I told you so."

A strong and exalted Moon may stabilise your mind in homely surroundings that have a calming effect on your mind, but you may also overly focus on the good things in life and attempt to avoid your darker moods and insecurities. Then, when the inevitable challenges arise, you may not feel prepared for them at all. If you never thought a negative thought, when something negative inevitably happens, you may not be as prepared.

Whatever the strength of the Moon in your birth chart, it's important to give your mind a sense of safety, while also preparing it for challenges. This requires adaptability, for which Rāhu is poorly equipped. If you are too extreme on either end of the spectrum of pleasure-seeking and avoidance versus negative thinking and catastrophising, you are unlikely living your best life. Even if your life is all good on paper, your feelings about your life may tell a very different story.

Rāhu's influence on the Moon is probably the most challenging of all. The Moon is said to be scared of Rāhu, just as the mind fears the shadows and all the demons that dwell within. You must look at your shadow, without overly focusing on what could go wrong or what stands in the way of your joy.

Find an inner joy that does not rely on outer circumstances or some elusive perfect setting.

Leo & 5th House

Rāhu in Leo or the 5th house can be a lot of fun, but fun is a spontaneous thing and Rāhu is anything but. Rāhu is the shadow part of you that is not usually present, so it's unlikely to be spontaneous. Yet it can show being hyperfocused at times, which can be very enjoyable and immersive, much like disappearing into a virtual world. Intelligence and intelligent decisions may be curtailed by overthinking or not thinking at all. The 5th house represents your confidence in making decisions, which may be a challenge with a shadow hanging around.

If you have children, another signification of the 5th house, you may obsess about them and actually push them away by trying to hold onto them too tightly. They will feel your fear for them whatever words you use, but if you also use fearful words there will be no doubt as to the impact it has on them. Ditto for lovers. Obsessing about a lover is only guaranteed to have one effect; that is, pushing the person you obsess over away. As ever, Rāhu is extreme on either side. At any rate, Rāhu is not about the person or thing you love, it's about the chase. You may unconsciously sabotage the very thing you seem to want, just so you can chase it again.

The Sun's strength and position will show how well you love and receive love, how you express yourself through your heart and creative endeavours, and whether or not children are an enjoyable experience or the bane of your life.

The Sun represents praise for what you do and who you are. The Sun's strength reflects how well you receive recognition and how much of a problem Rāhu may create in being viewed in a positive light. Whatever it is, it's never enough for Rāhu. You may be the head of the company, but you want to buy out another. You become famous for a, b, or c, but all you can think about is getting x, y, or z. You may have ten children but feel something is missing.

The Sun's strength and exaltation in Aries can show more confidence in expressing your creative side, and in how you project yourself into the future. While Rāhu is a block or bondage in some way, its association with a strong Sun can at least light a clearer path forward.

The Sun's weakness and debilitation in Libra may express itself as doubt in every move you make. You may not be confident and have low self-esteem, which only leads to more of a need for recognition. It doesn't matter how much you get, it's never enough. Ditto for children, lovers, or any kind of decision-making. If you are someone who invests and looks for power in the world of finances, Rāhu here may show great windfalls and even more dramatic falls you must be mindful of. 'Play the long game', as they say.

Whatever the strength and position of the Sun in your birth chart, Rāhu in Leo or the 5th house is about being clear about your future direction, either for your own plans and creative endeavours or for those of your children.

Virgo & 6th House

Rāhu in Virgo or the 6th house can cause, and then solve, lots of problems. You may obsess about problems and/or make improvements, depending. Rāhu is said to rule Virgo according to some Indian astrologers, bringing the desires of Rāhu down to earth in tangible ways. Although Rāhu here is ultimately beneficial for improving your daily routines and work schedule, it's not likely to promote service-orientated work unless there's something in it for you. This seems like a paradox, but Rāhu's higher expressions in signs it does better in is the ability to serve others, even humanity, while improving yourself. This could be a win-win situation if you are so inclined.

Rāhu in Virgo or the 6th house may show an obsession with illness and its treatments. If you get sick or know someone who is, you may focus solely on the illness but not enough on its alleviation. Ditto for problems with co-workers, employees, or competitors, as well as daily routines and habits. You may get so focused on what's not working and forget to keep a balance. You may focus so much on getting it right that you cannot let it go. In the end, you may end up with more problems than you solve, much like when someone attacks a problem head on before letting it work itself out in its own good time.

Rāhu can show great innovation and problem-solving, even if it must first show the problem in all its many variations. This is also an opportunity to come up with all kinds of solutions. The more open you can be to solutions, the better off you will be.

Relations with co-workers or employees would be impacted by Rāhu here, probably challenging you in some way so you can improve your work practices and skill set.

Mercury's strength and position will show how well you manage all the details, and if you overly focus on them or avoid them completely. Its strength and exaltation in Virgo can show an ability to take on the issues and deal with them effectively. You may do so in work by upskilling, for example, recognising that you do not have the adequate skills for the job. Or you may delegate tasks and problems, which is a strength of

Mercury in Virgo.

Mercury's weakness and debilitation in Pisces may show an inability to manage your work/life balance, exhausting yourself in the pursuit of an ideal, unable to find balance in the process of working things out. Yet Mercury in Pisces may also be reflected in an ability to 'think outside the box', so that you can approach problems in creative ways. As long as you are not avoiding issues because of feeling overwhelmed, there is the potential to see things from a bigger perspective, to find solutions that do not require hours of working it out in your head, leaving you mentally drained.

Libra & 7th House

Rāhu in Libra or the 7th house shows a lot of focus on relationships, maybe even an obsession about others. If you overly focus on the other, you are likely neglecting yourself. If you only think about fairness or a just cause, you may actually create an imbalance in the process.

You may have many relationships or marry more than once, not realising it is not about who you are relating with that Rāhu is interested in, but the need to chase someone. This can cause problems when you eventually wake up to the person you're with. Being in a relationship doesn't quench the insatiable thirst Rāhu has for more. You may sabotage the one you're with, just so you can chase another. Yet you're unlikely to be aware of this.

If you're not in a relationship, you may obsess about one, to the point you push people away. You may either jump impulsively into one, only to regret it later, sabotaging the relationship so you can find someone else. Yet you are unlikely to be aware of this tendency and probably blame them for it not working out. You may experience some extreme with others, a sense of overwhelm. They may indeed be overwhelming, but it is you that is allowing them in.

Venus' strength and exaltation in Pisces can help in being more compromising and loving, unconditionally. Yet Rāhu in Libra may challenge you to see others' points of view despite your more altruistic nature. They are *your* altruistic needs, after all. They may not be the needs of others. Rāhu in Libra can certainly give you what you desire, and this can help facilitate giving more to others. Yet it could also show an excessive focus on love and relationships that never satisfies an itch you cannot find to scratch.

Venus' weakness and debilitation in Virgo may add to the obsessive quality and fault-finding of Rāhu in Libra or the 7th house. Nothing or no one may satisfy your desire. This may lead you to seek out others who initially promise the earth but eventually disappoint. You may not feel appreciated for what you do or who you are. You're unlikely to do that for others. Praise may feel hollow, if indeed you receive or give any. If you are always fault finding, others are likely to do the same to you.

Scorpio & 8th House

Rāhu in Scorpio or the 8th house can challenge you to keep a healthy perspective and not dwell on dark thoughts all the time. You may catastrophise or, swinging wildly to the opposite extreme, attempt to ignore your problems. Either has their pitfalls. A gnawing sense of doom must be addressed, but you don't have to dwell on it all the time. You may have a therapist on speed dial and continually be going through a process. In overly focusing on processing trauma, you may simply be retraumatizing yourself. At the same time, you may not be dealing with life as you find it. You may not be clear about what needs to be done or dealt with appropriately. If you are always catastrophizing, you are unlikely to meet an uncertain situation with a rational mind, lessening your potential to see the issues clearly.

You may have a fascination with the macabre and not be able to take your attention away from it. You may find healthy ways to pursue these interests, so that it doesn't impact your life negatively. This is certainly a way to express an energy that's looking for attention.

Relationships with your partner's family may be one area you experience some challenge, either because of a lack of healthy boundaries, or many obstacles to overcome with them.

Mars' strength will show how you manage Rāhu in Scorpio. Mars' strength may show you courageously dealing with your issues. Yet Mars is a bit like Rāhu in that it doesn't know when to quit. Rāhu in Scorpio or the 8th house can further exaggerate Mars' tendency to be all or nothing. You may create as many, if not more, problems as you solve by dwelling on certain things.

A weak Mars may show you neglecting what you know you should do, just because you don't feel like it. By putting off appropriate responses, you may eventually explode inappropriately at someone who is clueless as to how you truly felt about the situation. A weak Mars may show an overcompensation that can express itself as a tyrant, pushing people around to find some sense of strength in uncertainty.

Control is an issue for Mars, whether strong or weak. And like all planets' strengths, sometimes a weakness can initially look like a strength. Rāhu in Scorpio will simply make things more extreme.

Sagittarius & 9th House

Rāhu in Sagittarius or the 9th house can bring up many complexities for all concerned. According to *Jātaka Pārijāta* (Subramanya 2008), the 9th house is not the best place for Rāhu. This is because Sagittarius and the 9th house are all about tradition, which Rāhu has no interest in. Rāhu is about the future and innovation, not tradition. But while I can see why an ancient Vedic culture would have viewed Rāhu in the 9th as a problem, I don't think it's as much of an issue in our modern era.

We're all encouraged to go it alone and forge our own path these days.

Rāhu in Sagittarius or the 9th house *can* show someone following a tradition, but it's just more likely to be obsessive and compulsive. This is not conducive to right-thinking, a crucial signification of the 'higher mind'. We used to rely on religion to steer us in the right direction in the past, but nowadays we're all left without proper guidance as to who or what to believe. This can bring great new perspectives, but it is just as likely to lead us astray.

Rāhu in Sagiitarius or the 9th house may show an intense hunger for knowledge that you end up confusing yourself with undigested tidbits. Speed reading a book is not going to allow you to fully digest the contents. The more you learn, the less you may feel you know. Travel and seeking out other cultures can show a neglect of where you came from and the wisdom of your birthplace and heritage.

Your relationship with your father probably had a profound effect on you, either because he was not there, or because he had poor boundaries. Yet he is simply a reflection of your own need to learn proper boundaries. This relationship is likely to have moulded your beliefs about what is possible even if you don't directly ascribe these beliefs to him.

Jupiter's strength and exaltation in Cancer can be of great benefit, as it keeps the waywardness of Rāhu at bay. Jupiter offers something to Rāhu it cannot muster on its own; that is, organization. Whether with your thoughts or your daily schedule, Jupiter's influence on Rāhu can be of great help in expanding your horizons without going astray. The more coherent your life is, the more you can learn and grow. The more chaotic your life is, the less likely positive growth occurs.

Jupiter's weakness and debilitation in Capricorn can show a lack of faith in whatever you are doing. Going it alone in a Rāhu period is already confusing, but Jupiter's weakness may leave you feeling completely lost as to what is the right thing to do. You may lack hope for a better future, and yet you may focus solely on what's next. You may not listen to anyone's advice, perhaps because those who attempt to advise you are not advisable to hang around with. But even if they are the most righteous guides, you are likely to bring out their worst.

Jupiter's weakness can show a lack of community support and a feeling of connection to others. Rāhu makes you feel disconnected, so it's vitally important to connect to something beyond yourself; something that is more than you, including something more meaningful than your selfish pursuits. You may not always be sure of what you are doing during Rāhu daśā, but you can keep striving for more knowledge, recognising it's never going to be enough.

Capricorn & 10th House

Rāhu in Capricorn or the 10th house can be a great place to focus on one of Rāhu's major significations; that is, ambition; in your career or some prominent role. But this brings up an interesting and contradictory impulse in a sign that's all about 'working for work's sake'. Rāhu is a part of you that is not interested in doing anything that does not reap some reward.

Rāhu may be more like your '15 minutes of fame', as opposed to long-lasting recognition or service to a cause that Capricorn epitomises. Capricorn prominent individuals usually like to work hard, but more so behind the scenes, so Rāhu here may make you feel uncomfortable with any spotlight. But spotlights offer more shadows to hide behind, I guess. You may find yourself hiding in others' fame, so some of it rubs off on you. Rāhu in Capricorn or the 10th house may hide your ambitions very well, even from yourself, protecting fame and position onto others. It may help to get on board with your own ambitions if you are to serve others' needs.

Saturn's strength can show detachment or sadness, depending. A strong and exalted Saturn in Libra is more likely to show a stoic and hard-working nature that pays off in the long term. Saturn's influence on Rāhu can help ground your ambitions in something real and is a stabilising effect on your lofty needs.

Saturn's weakness and debilitation in Aries may

show a lack of a strong work ethic and an inability to see something through to its conclusion. You may have many ambitions but realise none. This would only add to a sense of dissatisfaction Rāhu can instill. Even if you do achieve a great deal, you may either exhaust yourself or are unable to keep it going. A weak Saturn is not clear on healthy boundaries, whether work or personal. Rāhu has no boundaries at all. This can be a challenging mix unless handled carefully and deliberately.

Aquarius & 11th House

Rāhu in Aquarius or the 11th house can be powerful in a sign it is said to co-rule alongside Saturn. This can show great innovation and change that lasts. But it may also be reflected in not knowing for sure if the advancement that you achieve is for everyone's benefit or just your own. The advancement itself may not be for anyone's best interest, or there may be unintended consequences that you don't see right away.

Certainly, Aquarius or the 11th house of goal-setting is a great place to put Rāhu's ambitions. You just need to be mindful of not allowing your ambitions to block you from seeing the bigger picture, the impact your ambitions have on others, on society, even humanity. If you can channel Rāhu in Aquarius or the 11th house in a way that suits everyone, you're more likely to reap more benefits yourself. You're also more likely to achieve the kind of acclaim you crave deep down, whether you admit this or not.

Your friends and networks may have a big impact on you, as would older siblings, challenging you to bring your unique approach to the group, for the benefit of everyone. If not, you may find yourself ostracised by the group.

Saturn's strength and exaltation in Libra can ground any forward-thinking ideas in reality, making this a formidable duo to contend with. You know how to look beyond what is to achieve some new feat. Yet you know the rules of the game and how to play them, to get what you want. And you're more likely to compromise so everyone gets a cut.

Saturn's weakness and debilitation in Aries is likely to cause problems and blocks to your ambitions. You may not put in the hours that are needed or blame others for not cooperating. You may not see how to achieve your lofty goals. You may lack the appropriate resilience and give up at the first hurdle, of which there are likely more to deal with. You must accept that having bigger ambitions means having bigger and more problems to overcome.

Pisces & 12th House

Rāhu in Pisces or the 12th house may confuse you, as it is opposite Virgo, a sign it is said to co-rule according to some Indian astrologers. Rāhu in Pisces or the 12th house can show escapism or spiritual liberation, depending. And if you don't know how each of those differs, perhaps you've got Rāhu here! Escapism can come in the form of spiritual practices, what has been termed 'spiritual bypassing'. Yet Rāhu here can also show great insights and innovations that help all of humankind. You may be able to see beyond your own selfish needs or at least incorporate them into the bigger picture. Yet you may just as easily confuse yourself and others as to what is real. As usual, Rāhu can show extremes on both sides, and never more than in Pisces, a sign symbolised by two fish swimming in opposite directions. This highlights the need to incorporate the many different ways of feeling, and being, in the world.

A strong and exalted Jupiter in Cancer can help contain and explore the mystical realms despite Rāhu's distortions. You may be able to make real your lofty aspirations by letting go into the mystery of life a little more. You may be able to contain the insights and inspirations in a more helpful way for those in your community.

A weak and debilitated Jupiter in Capricorn may challenge you to see the rhyme and reason behind all the chaos and confusion that is possible with Rāhu in Pisces or the 12th house. You may doubt your role in the grand scheme of things, failing to see you are part of a whole and so much more than you can see.

Rāhu Conjoined Planets

Rāhu conjoins each of the planets as it transits each sign of the zodiac during Rāhu daśā, so you don't have to have Rāhu conjunct planets from birth to experience these conjunctions for a time. Rāhu and Ketu move around the zodiac every 18.5 years, transiting each Sun sign in a year and a half. Of course, if you have any planets conjunct Rāhu from birth you are more likely to resonate with these particular conjunctions when they take place again by transit. The themes of their conjunction in your birth chart are more likely to be triggered again when Rāhu transits back over the planet during your Rāhu daśā.

Rāhu & Sun

Rāhu conjoined the Sun can show extremes in your sense of self and need for recognition. You may not get the praise or platform you feel you deserve, but if you do, it probably won't satisfy you. There may be a sense of grandiosity that may not always be obvious. Someone playing the martyr can just as easily feel a type of grandiosity and position from playing the victim. The Sun represents the Self and a healthy self-esteem. Rāhu is a shadow, a false sense of self that obscures your true Self. This may express itself in seeking more validation from others, instead of the ideal internal validation you so need to develop. Social media intensifies these extremes, inflating and deflating you when you are the flavour of the month or have fallen out of favour.

Your father relationship may be strained or have poor boundaries. There may be some extreme in your relationship with him, either too much or not enough attention, which reflects these extremes in yourself.

The Sun in its highest expression represents pure presence, which you ideally achieve on your own. Yet the father may or may not have been present, whether physically present or not. This has a profound impact on your own ability to stay present.

You may undervalue or overvalue yourself, leading to irrational approaches to your skills and abilities. If you are successful, you may ignore all the others who have contributed to your success. If you are not, you may blame others for your shortcomings.

Whatever the house position of Leo, this area of life is likely to experience major ups and downs in Rāhu daśā. The highs can be extremely high, but the lows must be lower to counterbalance it. You may reach a high position but have doubts about your abilities to stay there. You may sabotage yourself because you don't actually believe in yourself. Any kind of bluster is simply showing you, and others, you do not believe in yourself. You need the validation from others and successes to keep you where you think you should be, where you deserve to be. Yet you may be unsure if you truly deserve anything you get. And anyway, external successes are simply unreliable. Life changes. People's tastes change. Success comes and goes.

You must develop a strong sense of Self with Rāhu combined with the Sun, connecting with an unshakable sense of confidence that comes from a connection that is internal and more elevated, beyond worldly success or failure.

Rāhu & Moon

The Moon is afraid of Rāhu, which devours it during an eclipse. The mind is afraid of shadows. The kind of distortion Rāhu presents challenges mental and emotional equilibrium. Yet this combination can show great insights into the human psyche, a great power and energy that can show a 'spirited' individual. The problems begin if the energy is not allowed a healthy outlet, leading to obsessive thinking and compulsive behaviour. Someone with this combination may develop many eccentricities and compulsions to help them cope with what feels like a threat, as they are constantly challenged to change their perception of what is possible.

Rāhu represents a constant alertness for signs of danger; and sometimes, faulty thinking that can lead to all kinds of inappropriate actions. Usually, Rāhu's obsessions are completely ill-conceived and out of place in a modern context. While Saturn is necessary, Rāhu is completely unnecessary. You probably don't have too much to worry about the horrors you dream up in your imagination, I wager. Yet Rāhu conjunct the Moon, either in your birth chart or by transit, can bring the mind to some dark places. It's important to place any fears or insecurities in context. Try not to lose perspective. If you do, at least acknowledge your unique perspective, and develop trust in others who probably have your best interest at heart. The issue with Rāhu-Moon is not trusting.

If you're overly focused on yourself, this combination can further disort your thinking. Your feelings of anxiety may fuel behaviours you would otherwise avoid. This may be why many with this combination have at least some idiosyncrasies. This is a need to channel anxiety through more productive means. It's too intense to sit with this kind of anxiety. You must do something with it.

If Rāhu is conjunct the Moon in your birth chart, and/or by transit while you experience Rāhu daśā, you can express your more spirited nature in ways that are more helpful. While it may seem helpful to join groups, these may further exaggerate negative thinking, such as social media platforms. It may be more helpful to find healthy routines away from artifical connections online to ones in the 'real' world.

One of the antidotes to Rāhu and modern life is to be in nature and to connect with the truth of this. Any kind of online environment is likely to further fuel negative thinking, even if it initially appears positive. Rāhu is a mask and people wear them more online.

Rāhu-Moon can go to even more extremes. This can express itself in paranoid delusions and mental disorders. Other Rāhu-type significations, such as drug use, may exacerbate these. While taking drugs or becoming addicted to any kind of substance or behaviour is an attempt to soothe oneself, it always ends up having the opposite effect.

The Moon shows how you feel, all the ways you feel. Rāhu-Moon can show a fear of feeling everything, which itself can lead to mental health issues such as depression and anxiety. Being anxious about being anxious or depressed makes it worse. Face your demons head on, and you will see that they only reside in your head. Someone who obsesses, has compulsions, or is hyperactive and unable to focus, or any other expression of Rāhu-Moon, repeats rituals for a reason. It's an attempt to cope with how they feel. Steadying the mind in nature is a great antidote to the chaos of Rāhu-type thinking.

Rāhu & Mars

This can be a tricky combination, as Rāhu is said to block Mars. Rāhu exaggerates. Mars represents your energy. This can lead to all or nothing. You may swing wildly from being energised to feeling completely flat. Mars is like a shot of expresso. Rāhu is like taking ten shots! The resulting jitters and nervousness can lead to ineffective energy output and actions. You may not be able to get anything done, either because you don't have the energy, or you have so much you cannot focus on one thing at a time. Either way, you are likely blocked from being productive. You may find you have so much focus and energy for a time but then spend it all in one sitting, leaving you without being able to focus at all.

The upside of this combination is the ability to do things differently to everyone else. While others may challenge what you are doing, perhaps with good cause, you may simply feel a compulsion you cannot ignore. If others do challenge you, use the challenge as just that: a challenge that can increase strength. Otherwise, you are likely to feel unable to do anything because of some sort of obstruction. Or you may get so much done you leave yourself exhausted and unable to cope.

Be mindful of how much your nervous system can take. Just as with the Rāhu-Moon combination, try to get out in nature and soothe yourself. Being by the sea is a great antidote to Rāhu-Mars. It cools and calms the nervous system, which can be on high alert with this combination. This will get you out of the fight or flight mode. Not everything is a competition. Yet you can use your competitive streak to achieve much.

Rāhu & Mercury

Rāhu's exaggerations and distortions can lead to overthinking and losing perspective. Yet Mercury can at least show an ability to discriminate fact from fiction. While you may experience overwhelm under this combination, you may at least keep enough emotional detachment so that you are not fueling faulty thinking.

You may not be able to 'see the wood for the trees' and may overly focus on all the many options to choose between. You may have several things on the go at the one time. Or you may simply think of many different things that you cannot let the mind rest in the now. Rāhu pushes a future agenda, where it seems everything you want is placed. But, in doing so, you may fail to see what is true now.

Depending on the strength of Mercury, you may manage this one well or become overwhelmed by all the factors involved. Making decisions may seem like a mammoth task when all of this is presented. The stronger the expression of Mercury, the more it tempers the chaotic impulses of Rāhu, leading to better discrimination. The more you can focus your mind on specific tasks, the better you'll be able to complete them efficiently.

Rāhu & Jupiter

This combination is termed *Guru Cāṇḍāla Yoga* in Indian astrology. *Guru* is the light, the truth, while *Cāṇḍāla* means an 'outcaste'. This can show a lack of clarity as to what is true, but also more innovative ways of looking at things. Jupiter shows truth without a need to figure it all out. It represents an 'inner knowing', or intuition. It reflects righteousness, which may be challenged by the shadows of Rāhu.

Although Jupiter is in many ways the antidote to Rāhu, when Jupiter is with Rāhu it too can become obscured. Faith in what is the right thing to do may be challenged by this combination. There may be a strong intuitive nudge, but you may not trust it. You may follow someone's advice but are led astray.

Depending on Jupiter's strength, this can challenge being able to see what's best. It could show complete and utter confusion as to how to progress. You may seek out advice from so many sources that you end up more confused than when you began to ask. This is telling you

you don't trust your own instincts and is reflected back to you in people who offer questionable advice. Asking one person for advice might help you confirm your own intuitions, but asking twenty different people is likely to lead you astray.

Whether a natal, and thus, lifelong lesson, or a temporary impact by transit, this combination can lead to many great insights. The problem is grounding them in reality and trusting where to take these new ideas.

Usually, a Rāhu-Jupiter connection by transit can lead to a break in the old ways of doing things and many great advancements. Yet Rāhu will also likely distort and obscure the truth of Jupiter, leading to a major shake-up. You may not organise your thoughts around these new ideas initially and must slowly integrate them once the coulds of confusion part.

Rāhu & Venus

This combination can be very enjoyable; probably, too enjoyable. But it can create a lot of issues in your finances and relationships. It may lead to indulgences. You may experience this as excess or depletion, depending. It may show one after the other, as and when sexual indulgence leads to depletion, or a shopping spree spends everything you have in the bank. Rāhu doesn't know healthy boundaries or balance, so you may end up having some extreme experiences that leave you worse for wear.

The upside of this combination is enjoying the

experiences it can bring along, including sensual and sexual enjoyment, relationships of all kinds, including with unusual people or those of a foreign culture, as well as many nice toys to play with if you play your cards right.

The issue with this combination is the darker side of Rāhu expressing itself through Venus. Rāhu pollutes Venus' purity. You may experience darker tones that can go to extremes, where you, or someone you are with, is not clear about what is a healthy boundary, sexually or otherwise. The word 'no' may not be in your vocabulary with this combination but must be learned so you don't go overboard and create problems for yourself, and everyone concerned.

Rāhu & Saturn

This combination can be one of the tricker ones for both Rāhu and Saturn. Rāhu's intensity and ambition can certainly be facilitated through the hard work of Saturn, but the problem is not feeling you are getting what you want as soon as you want it. Saturn asks you to work hard without immediate gratification. Even when you do get something out of all your hard work, you may not feel you have received your just rewards or the recognition for your part.

Rāhu is individualistic. Saturn represents responsibility towards others. Rāhu is the future, Saturn, the past. You may feel pulled in two directions at the same time. If you can channel your ambitions into something tangible and achievable, this can be a formidable duo. Otherwise, it can cause problems, as both battle it out for expression.

As always, it depends on their strength and position in your birth chart, or by transit. A weaker Saturn is unlikely to promote patience, as Rāhu eggs you on to achieve more, while Saturn pulls you back to your responsibilities. The pressures of Saturn, combined with the need for freedom with Rāhu, can be a tricky balancing act to maintain for any length of time.

Healthy boundaries are the core issue with this combination. You may have yours trampled on many times before you learn this.

This combination is even said to blur boundaries between this life and the next, with ghosts and spirits as one expression. While you may not see ghosts, you may feel like one. In other words, you may feel like your ambition is cutting you off from life, exhausting yourself and not leaving any time for simply living life and enjoying yourself. You may feel like the 'living dead' at times, running on an empty tank.

As with any Rāhu combination, it's important to find balance. This is often achieved by being in nature and natural surroundings, which can alleviate the Rāhu tendency to ignore what is in favour of what you would like to achieve.

Nine Phases of Rāhu Daśā

There are nine sub-periods within the 18 years of Rāhu daśā. Each sub-period or phase shows an underlying theme, bringing up its challenges and rewards. These nine phases combine Rāhu with the other 8 'planets' of Indian astrology in a way that is like a transit of Rāhu to one of these planets. In other words, if you are experiencing a Rāhu-Moon period, it's like having a Rāhu-Moon conjunction. Likewise, if you have Rāhu and Moon together in your birth chart, it's like experiencing a Rāhu-Moon daśā. This is a lifetime theme, as well as being especially prevalent during a Rāhu-Moon period.

Anyone who experiences the full 18 years of Rāhu daśā will also experience all the phases. Thus, it is like they experience the conjunction of Rāhu with all the planets. And indeed, they will, as Rāhu transits the entire zodiac in that time.

Rāhu-Rāhu

The first phase within the 18-year period of Rāhu is that of a sub-period of Rāhu itself. This lasts almost three years. This is the first bite of the apple, as it were. This is when the demon Rāhu first rears its head and may come as a complete and utter surprise to you. You may even use the word 'shocking' to describe this time in your life.

You will at least experience something that is out of your norm. This is perfectly normal during a Rāhu-Rāhu period. You may have someone enter your life you didn't expect or an event that you could never have predicted. In hindsight, this may seem obvious, yet Rāhu-Rāhu is usually a complex period where life goes in a completely different direction. Or you may fantasise about something you would never think of doing, and project it onto others who are doing it.

You are asking for this on some level, but you may not acknowledge this. You may wonder how on earth you have invited such things into your life. In doing so, you are missing an opportunity to recognise the potential and promise contained deep within you. Rāhu is pointing to some hitherto hidden part of you that therapists call your shadow. Whatever you call it, there is something that is coming up now for you to look at.

If you try to look away and point the finger at others or at things outside of you, you fail to see the opportunity for growth.

One of the problems with Rāhu is progressing too fast, too soon. You don't just take one bite of the apple; you devour the whole thing! You may take on more than you are able for or change your life way too dramatically for you to be able to adjust easily. You may not be conscious of doing this at all and focus on the upheaval on merely an external level, without acknowledging your inner need for change, for something else.

Stay open to the possibilities. Keep an open mind and you can take advantage of whatever is happening.

You may suddenly change residence or country, jobs or relationships. You may find yourself at a loss as to what to do next yet sense you cannot keep doing what you are doing. It's clearly time for a change, yet you may not see a way forward. You know you need to change, but you may not know what to do.

Progress is being made, even if it doesn't show up as something happening externally for some time. That is because Rāhu is not a physical planet and represents more of your psychological nature than anything else. Once your mind has been changed, which is what this period is all about, the changes are inevitable. And just like an eclipse, pointing to the inevitable changes, you too must make changes in your whole way of being in the world.

Rāhu-Jupiter

This period can be very expansive; but, whether expansion is a positive thing or not depends on your specifics. Most people experience a sub-period of Rāhu-Jupiter as a welcome return to sanity after Rāhu-Rāhu. Jupiter is the antidote to Rāhu and can calm it down. Being more organised, either because of some form imposed on you or by someone who is more organised in their thinking, such as a counsellor or adviser, or some organisation or institution, usually leads to a better situation.

It's time to take all those insights in Rāhu-Rāhu, after a period when life took you in a direction you hadn't accounted for, and settle down at this time. Yet Rāhu-Jupiter can also mean your life takes off in all kinds of ways.

Rāhu thinks big. Jupiter is literally the biggest planet in our solar system. Rāhu-Jupiter combined multiplies all the opportunities and possibilities. It can be a heady mix of potentials. You may have big plans at this point; but, without being organised, you can forget about doing anything about them. The more orderly you can be at this stage, the more you can channel the oftentimes chaotic revelations of Rāhu into something more meaningful and purposeful.

The more organised you are, the more growth you will experience. Growth cannot occur without an organising principle or influence at work in the background. Jupiter highlights a sense of a stillness in the background of life's ups and downs, holding space for all the potential that is ripe now.

Rāhu-Saturn

This period can be one of the most–if not the most-complicated and conflicted within the entire Rāhu daśā. Yet it can also be when you are your most successful, on paper, at least. This is because, whatever Rāhu ambitions have begun to settle in you now, Saturn is the ability to focus and make it happen. Yet Saturn is also the wall you must negotiate, the full stop that says you cannot do anymore than you are doing.

You are likely to keep going despite the sense you need to slow down. Rāhu eggs you on. Saturn slows you down. How can you give voice to both? It's not easy, but it's a time to recognise your ambitions while doing what you must right now. It may not satisfy the Rāhu impulse, but you must learn to balance your ambitions with your responsibilities. Otherwise, the two conflicting impulses–one pushing you forward, the other pulling you back–is likely to exhaust you.

These two 'planets' are seen by most Indian astrologers as the most 'malefic' of the lot, so having both active at the same time can challenge even the most stoic individual. Yet there are more rewards here than elsewhere. The more you can channel your ambitions into patient work and precision, the better off you'll be. This is likely to be the making of you, although you are unlikely to feel that way about it at this stage. You're more likely to wish to avoid what you cannot. The more you avoid the issues, the harder they become. Saturn is asking you to deal with your life, as it is, whatever Rāhu is telling you you should be doing.

Everything has its time. Saturn's time-period shows up as suffering due to the consequences of past thoughts, words, and actions which were not advantageous for those on the receiving end of those thoughts, words, and actions in the past. You cannot avoid the pain as a result. Thus, Saturn could be seen as necessary pain. The pain of Rāhu, on the other hand, is completely unnecessary. It's all in your head.

This period can either make or break you. It's probably going to break you to put you back together again in a more fragile, more humbled, more real state. The more real you become, the more you can achieve. You will not be the same ever again. The ego takes a beating in the months and years of a period of Rāhu-Saturn and yet something more important is born within you.

Saturn is a clearing out of any unnecessary baggage, a cleansing of any pain that was not felt in the moment. Any emotional baggage is due to be dropped once Saturn ripens. Yet you may only be aware of the pain and form a new identity based on it.

The dropping of any defenses in order to release pain may prove to be the ego's downfall and the soul's cry to be heard. Saturn teaches you many things, but mostly it teaches you how to let go. Rāhu-Saturn teaches you to let go of your ambitions, your obsessions, everything that is not real.

Rāhu-Mercury

This period can be a time of recovery if the Rāhu-Saturn has taken its toll. It's time to build yourself up again, like a house that has been laid bare and needs a refit. It may be a time you go back to school or upskill in your current position. You're probably more willing to engage with others, after a more solitary period of Rāhu-Saturn. Mercury likes to play with ideas and choices, of which there are likely many at this stage.

The downside as always with Rāhu is overdoing it, leaving little room for rest, leading to more imbalances, this time, overstimulation and mental agitation. There may be a lot of choices to choose between in Rāhu-Mercury and, although you are likely to welcome these after having little or no choice in Rāhu-Saturn, it's likely to be too stimulating and confusing at times.

The good news is that you've probably begun to settle into this Rāhu thing at this stage. If Mercury is strong in your birth chart, you may be able to be more practical and plan your future. As options open up for you, it's a time to make full use of them, while keeping an eye on what you are here to do in the first place. Try not to get too distracted by the many opinions and things happening in your life now and simply focus on what you are meant to be doing with your time.

By all means, enjoy this period, but try to limit your exposure to media and others' points of view, as these will further stimulate an already overstimulated mind. The inevitable mental exhaustion can lead to not being able to discriminate between what is true and false.

Rest as much as you can, while doing all you can during this highly productive period.

Rāhu-Ketu

This is the mid-way point in the whole 18-year Rāhu daśā. For that reason, it's a pivotal and crucial time. It may be experienced as the eye of the storm by some, while others may rally everything against the timeout that is required. For many, Ketu can bring loss, which brings with it a full stop in some experience. This may be upsetting, but it's also an opportunity to be still.

Rāhu is chaotic at the best of times, while the previous Rāhu-Mercury period is usually overly stimulating. Rāhu-Ketu asks you to shut off for a while, to be still, but not like Rāhu-Saturn, which asked you to show up and work hard. Rāhu-Ketu asks the real "you" to show up, i.e., your spiritual self, the one who is keeping an eye on proceedings, whatever is going on. The more you can tap into the 'part' of you that never changes in the midst of the most changeable and transformational period of your life, the better off you'll be. If you cannot tap into your spiritual essence, it's likely Ketu will confuse the hell out of you. You're likely to be at least a little confused and uncertain as to what to do next. Ketu is not about any experience. It's simply the experiencer. It asks you to become aware of who or what is aware in the first place. For most people, this means removing things or people from their life that kept them in the experience.

Yet Rāhu continues to push its agenda, whatever that is for you specifically, during Rāhu-Ketu. Now, Ketu kicks in to remind you of the You that was here before the small you got on board and hijacked the show. It's a year-long period where you are asked to let go of something so you can deepen your experiences.

The more you can relinquish something at this stage, either a relationship, a sense of who you are, a job or whatever, the more you can free yourself for what comes next. What comes next is usually more enjoyable, i.e., Venus. As one client conveyed to me, "It was like a soft landing after being in freefall."

Rāhu-Venus

Although Venus can offer great enjoyment and comfort after a perplexing period of Rāhu-Ketu, it can bring up its own issues, as anything mixed up with the shadow of Rāhu can. One of the more obvious pitfalls of this period is not being satisfied with your life or your partner. If you're not partnered, you may crave one.

You may think the 'grass is greener' if you do, only to find out that doesn't satisfy you either. Although some astrologers state that this period can signify the end of a relationship, I have not always seen this to be the case. It depends on the particulars of the person's chart; how mature you are.

A weak or afflicted Venus can be further challenged by Rāhu, but this doesn't mean you cannot work through the issues. The key is to recognise they are your issues, not your partners, or anyone else. Rāhu is *your* shadow. There's no one to blame here, including yourself.

In a way, you cannot ignore the call to indulge something in Rāhu-Venus, but you can be more conscious of what you are doing, and why you are doing it. What hole are you trying to fill? You may have to 'go there' to learn the lesson that it's never enough. Either way, this is usually a turning point in your relationships and what you value.

Rāhu-Sun

This period heralds the waning cycle of Rāhu in many ways, the beginning of the last three sub-periods within the whole Rāhu daśā. It will take a few years for the shadows to do their thing, of course. You may feel you are over it, but Rāhu is not done with you yet!

There are many more shadow dynamics to work through in the waning cycles of Rāhu daśā, in Rāhu-

Sun, Rāhu-Moon and Rāhu-Mars. And just like the beginning of Rāhu daśā during Rāhu-Rāhu, the ending phases have their own intensity and complexity.

If you have lived long enough, it's at this point that the past comes back in various guises, to help you assimilate and understand it, to call back your projections so you can become whole. In other words, if you have already experienced a major period of Sun, Moon, and Mars previously, Rāhu now combines with these for new insights and revelations.

Rāhu-Sun may bring up all kinds of interesting dynamics in terms of one's sense of self. You may seek validation at this time, impressing yourself on the world around you. Yet you may not feel fulfilled no matter how much you project yourself onto the world; no matter how much success you achieve.

Rāhu-Sun can exaggerate and distort your sense of self out of all proportion, including what you think you are capable of. You may promise much, but underdeliver. Life might do the same. The thing is to understand where your true source of power and position comes from. It is not in a role in any worldly sense. If that is your definition of power, then power is fleeting, as all roles must be relinquished in the end. But it doesn't mean you shouldn't chase success and recognition at this stage. You can do so, as long as you are connected to the truth of who you are beyond all roles and titles.

The father relationship may come into sharp focus

at this time, as you unravel some of the dynamics with such a figure in your life. If that has been a challenge in your life in general, it's now that the dynamics may reach a head. It's time to get clear about this relationship, or lack thereof, so you can find the power and majesty in your own being, to become who you were always meant to be.

Rāhu-Moon

This is the penultimate phase of the whole Rāhu daśā, and perhaps a complex time because of it. It is further complicated by the fact that the Moon is what is eclipsed by Rāhu. Your mental and emotional state may be in great flux at this time. It's important to keep things in perspective and recognise when you are blowing things out of proportion. Rāhu exaggerates, so if there are pleasant emotions, it can be very enjoyable. The problem is that pleasant things are always counterbalanced with unpleasant feelings.

The higher you go, the lower you go.

Pleasure and pain are two sides of the same coin, one which continually flips in your mind. The Moon reflects your constantly changing state of mind, your likes and dislikes. Rāhu further intensifies this flipping from one to the other, and why being more temperate and level-headed is advisable. Of course, that's not what you're likely to experience during Rāhu-Moon. Go with the flow of how you are feeling, without repressing anything, but also without indulging any fantasies. Oftentimes, fantasies may take on a darker tone, as you subject your mind to the shadow aspects. But if you can face up to your fears, you realise there is nothing to fear but fear itself.

Further problems arise if you are afraid to feel the full gamut of your emotions. If you attempt to wrestle your feelings into submission, you're likely to end up with more problems. It's time to face whatever feelings you have hitherto repressed, so you can integrate them and move on. You cannot move on with a more determined mindset if some vague feeling in the background plagues you. Address the issues and you'll be more proactive in the next and final phase of Rāhu.

Rāhu-Mars

This can be a complex period, just as any ending phase within any major period can be. A major part of your life is ending, something in your life is changing. Rāhu-Mars has the potential to be even trickier as both of these energies battle it out.

The sub-period of Mars points you back to the previous major Mars cycle, many Moons ago, before your ego got out of hand in Rāhu daśā. This is important to note, as the one thing Rāhu and Mars have in common is a sense of selfishness and ego, which exists to defend you against attack. Yet this sense of self is a fabrication, on some level, as Rāhu's artificial nature, infused with Mars's need for independence and control, leads to all kinds of power dynamics you may not be able to manage as easily. It may be a challenge to simply view life and experiences, especially other people, as anything other than a threat to your survival. Keep things in perspective.

Be mindful of when you overly identify with your egoic needs, which may blow perceived threats out of all proportion. At the same time, there is a need to gain power and control over the beast that is Rāhu, finally. It's a tricky balance to keep, but if you can both allow the energy free reign at times, while reining it in at others, you're more likely to manage this period better.

As challenges rear their heads in Mars's period, in the context of shadow elements you must finally master, you may either feel more equipped to deal with your inner demons or attempt to run away. It all depends on your relationship to your own power and autonomy, and how well you have thus far integrated your shadow.

However well you manage it, this last phase of Rāhu daśā is just that, an ending, and should be treated as such. Whatever old foes or challenges rear their heads, even if it's simply inside your head, this is just a steppingstone to something else. Try not to hold onto anything.

It's a good idea to take whatever is presented with a pinch of salt, knowing that a new horizon awaits you in Jupiter's major period. This begins once Rāhu and Mars have squeezed every last drop of ambition out of you. For that reason, it's best not to take on any more than is necessary at this stage. Instead, use all your energy, which is likely to spike and dip dramatically, to finish as many projects and things in your life. Of course, this all depends on where Mars is and what it rules in your birth chart, as well as its position in relation to Rāhu itself. Whether Mars acts as a friend or foe, this is a time to be challenged one last time before you can experience the blessings of Jupiter.

As Rāhu takes its leave over the year of Rāhu-Mars, feel the intensity one last time, as you eventually realise the letting go of fear, or whatever limitation you feel, leads you to new possibilities for growth and repair in Jupiter daśā.

Kālsarpa Yoga

The study of Rāhu and Ketu is the most profound aspect of horoscope analysis: the story of Rāhu, the head of the demon Svarbhānu in Vedic myth, and Ketu, the headless body, both representing two dynamic forces at opposite ends of our evolutionary spectrum-where we are coming from (Ketu) and where we feel compelled to move towards (Rāhu).

Yet the first few years of Rāhu daśā can be particularly volatile, with lots of change happening outside of your conscious awareness. The middle part of the daśā, i.e., Rāhu-Ketu, can be just as complex. By Rāhu-Ketu, the mid-point in Rāhu daśā, all the big themes of the lunar nodes, and your life, come to a head, and your life may change in more profound ways. Even if your outer circumstances don't seem to change, you are likely to change your outlook and then life lines up with your new perspective.

This process can be more complex, as Rāhu and Ketu being active at once churns things up and flips things around. Something new is born in you, but something old has to die. This may feel like the shedding of a skin and why Rāhu-Ketu are likened to serpents in Vedic myth.

The difference between Rāhu and Ketu is important. Rāhu is correlated with the lower serpentine energy, deified as *Sarpas*, while Ketu correlates with the *Nagas*, a higher vibration of the serpent deities.

The lower vibration Sarpas bring out all the things we associate with serpents, including sneaking about in the shadows, being sly, etc. Nagas are the more evolved serpent deities, which can elevate you to more enlightened states. Yet according to Sadhguru, "Naga always has to be backed up by something. It is not an energy of itself. It's a perception. It is receptive." This is essentially the reflection of the lunar nodes and their need for a host planet. You must never take either node in its sign and house position without considering the state of the planet that rules the sign.

Kālsarpa Yoga is said to occur when all the visible planets, Sun, Moon, Mars, Mercury, Jupiter, Venus and Saturn, line up on one side of the 'nodal axis'. The side on which they line up makes all the difference. When the planets line up on one side so that the progressed planets would meet with a retrograde Rāhu, it is specifically named Kālsarpa Yoga. When they line up on the opposite side, moving towards Ketu, it is named *Kālamṛta Yoga*.

While both have the tendency to show extremes, highlighting, for better or worse, all of the themes presented in this book, Kālsarpa Yoga may be more challenging, simply because Rāhu is more involved with the planets' transits. If you were born with this combination, Rāhu would have subsequently transited all your natal planets.

Even if you don't have it in your birth chart, Kālsarpa Yoga happens from time to time, whenever the slower moving Jupiter and Saturn line up together. It's then just a matter of time before the faster-moving planets join them. For those who experienced this at birth, it means it's a recurrent theme throughout their life. But it also means there is likely a turning point in their lives, as if their life seems to move in the opposite direction.

Kālsarpa Yoga may show Rāhu-related themes are the catalyst for a major turning point at some point. They may be materialistic for some time, or wish for some success in some way, but then switch to being more spiritually focused.

Although the Kālamṛta Yoga is seen as less challenging, it depends on how you look at it. Yes, the ultimately goal of Ketu is liberation, reflecting a need to renounce the world altogether, but someone may not have this as a conscious impulse. Thus, the planets being devoured by Rāhu's counterpart Ketu may actually show more loss, in a worldly sense, at any rate.

Kālamṛta Yoga is seen as more beneficial because at least the person may turn to something beyond this world for solace, finding peace there, while someone focused solely on success and Rāhu's ambitions may continue to struggle with the entanglement.

Kālsarpa Yoga is a controversial topic in Vedic astrology, mainly because it is not found in any classical texts. True to form, the shadowy nature of the lunar nodes takes a firmer hold when we ignore them. There is indeed reference to this yoga in Tantrik texts that appear later in South India.

The lunar nodes themselves are full of controversies, paradoxes, and uncertainties. They are shadows that darken the mind. Sometimes, these shadows offer a different perspective which brings great insights. At other times, they completely obscure reality. Sometimes conspiracy theories are onto something. Yet they often take that something and distort it.

When shadows impact all the planets, they become even more potent, and yet subtly so. The subtler something is, the more powerful. Because we are not aware of it, it has more of an impact. This formation can often show us feeling out of control, as the shadows works in the background, just like serpents.

The lunar nodes represent our hidden nature, things which confound, things we reject. And yet, they also fascinate us. And just like conspiracy theories, there is much controversy and polarizing opinions about them. Everything lines up on one side, showing a divisive, lopsided view.

The Kālsarpa or Kālamṛta Yogas bring a sense of time being warped, looped and extreme, creating a sense of instability. This instability creates more change, along with the instability. Yet it moves things along all the same.

Rāhu continues to point us forward, grasping for something we feel we lack, as we try to fill a void, represented by Ketu, the south node. Ketu points us back, to where we come from, in our lives, and in a spiritual sense; the emptiness to which we all return one day, the 'void' or 'non-self' spiritual folk speak of.

We tend to reject this in a worldly sense, just as we don't like to think of our own death; our minds somehow tricking us into avoiding the subject. When it does come to visit, when someone close to us dies, we are left feeling shocked. We feel the void they leave behind. Yet Ketu also represents the connection we all have to one another, through this void.

Ketu represents mistakes, as our past is full of them! This often pulls our awareness back to look at where we went wrong. Yet we often keep doing the very thing we wish to overcome because it becomes our default mode. Because we are so focused on the future, on Rāhu, we keep repeating the same old mistakes, missing the lessons the past is teaching us.

You can blame Rāhu daśā for that too, as it keeps

pulling you forward, pushing its/your agenda. Wishing for something in the future keeps you moving away from your past. You will step over anyone to get what you want when the serpent has a hold of you.

By becoming aware of your shadow nature, you can begin to integrate the shadows. You can override the need to "transcend too soon", as Ken Wilber describes, poorly integrating what you wish to get over. This tendency creates the shadows, as you overshoot the mark and fail to integrate the experience. You eventually get tripped up and slip back down. In the process, you set up another type of shadow. As Wilber explains when asked in an interview, if something goes wrong in the inclusion (Ketu), "it gets split off and [you] can get addictions to that" (IntegralZen 2018). It's unconscious, so you remain stuck to it. You develop two types of shadow: 1) going too far and 2) not going far enough, or what Wilber refers to as "addictions and allergies", i.e., Rāhu and Ketu.

Wilber calls these our "subpersonalities" that have been pushed out of our awareness. This takes some of our energy and awareness with it, "down to the basement", leaving us feeling less and less authentic. Yet there is potential here to become more authentic, as indeed you eventually must become. The more you can integrate the parts of you that are split off, the more authentic you become during Rāhu daśā.

The past influences the future. The future influences the past.

This loop is never more impressed then when someone has a Kālsarpa or Kālamṛta Yoga at birth. You can clearly see the past influencing your future, but your future also influences your past. What you do in the future reframes your past. How you feel in any given moment changes the way you see the past. On and on it goes - life, that is, propelling you forward (Rāhu), showing you the results in time (Ketu). On and on it goes, like a loop you're stuck in and cannot begin to think how you can escape, as you don't even know you are trapped in the first place.

Snakes & Ladders

Have you ever played the board game Snakes and Ladders? It is a great teaching tool for life, actually. This is what it was first used for. Surviving game boards suggest Snakes and Ladders emerged somewhere in Northern India or Nepal, where the game was known as the 'Game of Knowledge'.

You get so far up the ladder, but at the roll of the dice (karma), you find yourself slipping down the snake. You take one step forward, and then slip ten steps back. Sometimes, you take just one step forward and then are catapulted many levels up the ladder. Great! Yes, but then you eventually meet with another snake. Big life lessons right there!

Everything is a reaction to everything else. That is all the word karma means, i.e., action. But the word *kārmik* may be applied more to the nodes because they are shadows, and shadows operate outside our conscious awareness for the most part. And as Carl Jung is quoted as saying, ""Until you make the unconscious conscious, it will direct your life and you will call it fate." So, Rāhu-Ketu can feel more fated, more kārmik. However, on some level, however unconscious, you are making it happen. It's just not the you you think of as you that is.

Kālsarpa Yoga, or any variation, any kind of Rāhu extreme, be it with the Sun or Moon, or many planets, may feel like you are getting somewhere extremely fast initially, as if playing a game of Snakes and Ladders. But eventually, you slip back down the snake to where you were, maybe even further back down. To get ahead in life, you may feel you must jump over something, or someone, only to find it's what trips you up later.

Age of ~~Aquarius~~ Narcissus

Rāhu and Aquarius express individuality, innovation, and ambition. They push things forward. Yet one of the dichotomies of Aquarius is the possibility of rigid thinking, despite its innovative approach. It can show getting stuck in negative thoughts, which may benefit from the use of drugs, or even hallucinogens (another signification of Rāhu), to break free. An example of this in recent times is the use of psilocybin to treat anxiety and depression in therapeutic settings.

The increase of mental illness is clear in our modern era. But what's not so obvious is where this is coming from. It seems to be all about disconnection. And for that, we can look to another signification of Rāhu and Aquarius: technology. It's the disconnection created by something that paradoxically should connect us to one another that is at the heart of the problem, it seems. And this is where narcissism turns up-not only as a fixation and promotion of the individual, but because of a sense of disconnection from others.

A sense of disconnection is what lies at the heart of all our fears. And when we disconnect from one another, and from the natural world, a trend which is likely to increase exponentially in the years to come, we are likely to be left feeling anxious, isolated, desperate for connection–to anything. I don't think the coming age is as *The 5th Dimension* sang about. But while I don't think it's all bad, there are some challenges.

Narcissism may not be what most of us think of when we think of someone without empathy, of someone focusing solely on themselves. Or the 'dark triad' of narcissism, Machiavellianism, and psychopathy; traits of which could easily apply to more extreme expressions of Rāhu. It may be a need that springs from an inability to connect to something greater, within. When we connect with something greater, we no longer want to connect to something which feels like an imposter: the ego, in a negative sense, Rāhu, the shadow.

In an era that promotes individuality and a strong media presence, darker Rāhu themes can run rampant. And if we are not aware of our shadow, it can take a stronger hold, wrapping itself around us until we can no longer see truth from falsehood, let alone claim enlightenment.

But don't worry about it, as you can now plug into a device! Ultrasound devices that help transcend everyday consciousness are perhaps a positive expression of the use of technologies. We seem to be living in a 'hyperreality', with AR, VR, AI, Deepfakes and 'Deep States'. Aquarius as the bādhaka, the blocker, hides things in our psyche, and in plain sight, in society. If it has been shown in some art form, it's a possibility. Someone, somewhere, dreamt it up in their imagination. It already exists. It just needs to be grounded in reality, in Saturn, the other ruler of Aquarius.

Rāhu and Saturn may have a sign in common, but they have many differences, with one promoting stability (Saturn) and one progress and change at every turn (Rāhu). But what they do have in common is a mistrust of anyone in power. Rāhu may show a yearning for connection, but it questions any kind of authority and wise council in favour of working it out all on its own. This leads to a disconnect from any tradition, spiritual or otherwise.

"Narcissism in the birth chart seems to be particularly acute when Rāhu occupies bhava [houses] 1-6-10-11", according to Barbara Pijan Lama (Pijan Lama 2023). I would add the 3rd house to this list. Rāhu is said to do well in houses 3-6-10-11. These are the places of growth and improvement, which means Rāhu can promote its wishes here. But before you go checking your birth chart and find it in one of these, take heart that Rāhu's narcissistic impulse can always be elevated to the best of what Aquarius has to offer; that is, a wish to help others get what you want, to live in a society that benefits everyone.

Age of Aquarius Timeline

There are a lot of opinions about when the actual Age of Aquarius begins. I've heard of dates ranging from 2117 to 2600. Many astrologers believe it has already begun, and for some time.

'The Great Year' is the time it takes the Equinoxes to precess through the zodiac, in 25,772 years. Thus, each of the 12 signs are 2,147.5 years in length. Whatever way you look at it, this is the dawning of a new age. Pisces may still be where the Sun rises on the northern spring Equinox, but Aquarius is the sign you see on the horizon at sunrise.

Doug Egan writes in an article on *Astrology News Service* website (Egan 2017), "if the weather forecaster on TV is telling you that it is sunny, but you look outside and it is pouring down rain, it's probably more appropriate to go with the rain. Regarding the Age of Aquarius: perhaps we are already in it."

The rise of Rāhu and fall of religions is apparent, but is atheism a type of 'stealth religion'? God in the Piscean form seems to be ending, as religion and tradition are thrown out in favour of progress. Aquarius is twelve houses away from Pisces, the sign of faith. This means a loss of faith, of religion, a loss of belief in the existence of a higher order. But God is not dead. God is the new tech! Tech is everywhere, in everything we do, and to be worn by everyone as a device in the future. So, we're always going to be connected to the God of Technology!

Other Aquarius themes include non-binary genders, as Saturn co-rules Aquarius alongside Rāhu and is seen as a 'neuter' planet.

Some dichotomies we can observe with Aquarius are a need for order *and* disorder, individuality within communities, freedom within restrictions. All of these apparently opposite themes are reflected in the opposing forces of Saturn and Rāhu. Saturn is the planet of form and structure, while Rāhu is formless, without boundaries.

In the Age of Aquarius, we are likely to move beyond current boundaries, of what we thought was possible. We must shore up our personal boundaries as things around us change in more extreme ways. As technology improves our lives, it may also be challenging to assimilate into our being.

We can find ways to cope with the advancements. We can evolve and make use of technology that is apparently evolving faster than we can digest. We can move beyond our unconscious conditioning and evolve beyond narcissism, into a more assimilated whole, while keeping our individual selves intact.

As Kishori reminds me, we are the wave that crashes back into the ocean.

Tomorrow's People Today

My astrology teacher, Pearl Finn, used to refer to Rāhu as 'Tomorrow's People'. I understood this at the time, before I had entered Rāhu daśā, but I truly get it now. Rāhu pushes boundaries. It pushes our buttons, too. Yet without doing so we cannot progress. Rāhu represents the creators and innovators, the disruptors, in our society, and in us.

We need people like this in society to challenge the status quo; as, even if the status quo were appropriate at one time, it cannot be so forever. Things must progress for that to become the status quo one day, a status quo which must be challenged.

Neurodivergents

Neurodivergent individuals, those whose brain differences affect how their brain works, challenge the status quo. They change systems that are put in place for 'neurotypicals'. They require a new kind of system that addresses their needs, until one day, they are the norm and other neurodivergent individuals push the boundaries yet again. This is how humanity progresses.

This is happening on a societal level over millenia, of course. We don't notice it too much. But when you enter a Rāhu daśā, you experience a drastic shift in your life. You take a quantum leap.

If you have previously identified with a spectrum of some kind, Rāhu daśā can push you further up the scale. If you don't, it's likely you will find new ways of looking at the world, and of operating within it.

Once I had a good portion of Rāhu daśā behind me, I felt I could identify more with autism.

Have you noticed an increase in people being diagnosed as being on the autism spectrum in recent years? Or ADHD? That's not a coincidence. We are moving into an Age of Aquarius, after all. Rāhu as co-ruler of Aquarius highlights these kinds of divergent ways of thinking and being in the world.

I've noted the great potential in this, not just the obvious challenges. If you've ever noticed your mind wandering off after a period of 'hyper-focus', this is a Rāhu-type experience. Rāhu is all or nothing; hyperfocus, and then not being able to focus at all.

This is likely to increase in an Age of Aquarius, an age of technological advancement that is likely to distract us even more with immersive technologies. As we're all plugged into a system, it robs our attention span. Social media and wearable tech are just the beginning, so we better get on board with managing our time and attention in the years that follow.

At one point, I wanted to do a study of Rāhu in the charts of those who identify with ADHD, but I didn't get around to it!

The autism spectrum is a good example of a Rāhu-type experience; a need to disconnect from others when feelings of overwhelm rise up. Much like the hyperfocus and then lack of attention of someone with ADHD, autism reflects the extremes of Rāhu through intensely sensitive individuals. They soothe themselves with obsessive rituals. They appear to have no empathy and are only focused on themselves. But this is a misunderstanding of their intense sensitivity to others, which leads to a need to disappear into their own world.

Autism is something I began to consider for myself towards the end of my Rāhu daśā; although, if I am 'on the spectrum' I would probably be labelled as 'high functioning autistic', which is currently referred to as 'autism spectrum disorder', and previously, Asperger's syndrome. I think it's helpful for anyone in Rāhu daśā to look to those on the autism spectrum to understand some of the dynamics, regardless. Rāhu is a mask, and those on the spectrum tend to mask more. Rāhu daśā can increase this need, but it also highlights the need to take the mast off. Rāhu helped me see I may have been masking my whole life.

Rāhu makes everything more extreme, so we cannot ignore the issues any longer. If you see yourself as being neurodivergent in any way, Rāhu daśā is likely to make it seem more so; although, whether you should pathologise yourself is another matter.

Social interactions and communications can be overwhelming, especially if Rāhu is placed in houses, 1, 2, 3, 7 or 11. Everything about Rāhu is overwhelming. That's the point. Whether you are on a spectrum, or whether Rāhu daśā has made it feel that way, it's your experience that counts. Labels have their place if they help you manage your life and not hinder you if they become unhelpful self-fulfilling prophecies. Yet labels do help you externalise what's happening, allowing you to deal with the situation more objectively. This is usually of help in Rāhu daśā.

Having a structured life, whether you identify with ADHD or autism, is of great help in Rāhu daśā.

Primal Fear in a Modern World

Rāhu is the fear that some core need is not *going to* be met. Note 'going to' as the most important phrase in that statement. You're likely okay where you are right now, reading this. But that doesn't stop your mind wandering off into an imagined future, where you may be on a low-grade alert for potential dangers. That kind of alertness may have suited an ancient person protecting themselves from predators, but it is unlikely to be helpful to you on an ongoing basis in your modern life. Worse still, you're probably also subjecting your mind to an endless amount of threats via news media. And you're probably sitting on a comfortable chair while you do. You are not likely to be working these experiences through your nervous system, discharging the energy. Watching shocking scenes on a screen, whether fact or fiction, your nervous system cannot tell the difference. Add to this a sense of lack, even though you probably have everything you'll ever need. Rāhu will make it feel like you won't survive without x, y or z. It's a primal thing. It all comes down to fear. You may fear missing out, or not having enough. However unrealistic, Rāhu can bring a sense of threat to your survival.

The emotional brain takes over rational thought. Rāhu daśā can show you on constant alert for modern-day predators, which gives you a hint to the best antidote. As much as you can, stay away from media or anything online that makes you fearful. You don't need it. You can be informed, ideally, by a level-headed individual, but you don't need to be inundated.

Yoga practices, whether physical postures or breathwork, is a great antidote. Being in nature is another. See the chapter on *Antidotes* for more remedial measures you could adopt.

Understand: Rāhu is like the part of your brain, your amygdala, which is there to keep you alive. Problems arise when you cannot shut off or reduce the alert to threat levels, even when there are none. And let's face it, most of the threats you will face in life are located between your ears. While this is a powerful mechanism that keeps you safe in one way, it's not appropriate in most situations and leads to feelings of lack, depleting your energy.

Yet you cannot argue with it, as it's a part of your brain that doesn't think – it reacts unconsciously. You just need to manage it better during Rāhu daśā.

Healing Poison

Some people might say that we can 'choose our poison'. I disagree. Just look to the position of Rāhu in your birth chart and tell me you have a choice in the matter. And if you feel you have, then you haven't begun your Rāhu daśā yet. Get back to me when it's over! And don't be fooled into thinking your poison isn't a poison, even if it were a healthy activity to begin with. Even meditation can be someone's poison if used to avoid dealing with some issue that needs attention. You can get high on that stuff!

By acknowledging your need for a poison, whether a substance, experience, or state of being, you can actually use it to heal yourself. A little bit of poison does wonders. Too much and you're unlikely to be able to cope.

If you have Rāhu in the 10ᵗʰ house of career, it may be a good idea to ask yourself if you truly need another promotion. Is it worth the price you have to pay? If you've got Rāhu in the 2ⁿᵈ house, do you really need that extra slice of cake?

But what does a little bit of posion look like? Perhaps a little bit of what you fancy, even if you cannot admit to yourself, let alone others, that you want such a thing. I'm not suggesting you indulge every whim. I'm referring to something that constantly plagues you. You may consciously state it is not what you want, and yet it keeps showing up in your life experience. This is what it means to 'face your shadow.' Look to the person or thing that is triggering you in a strong way and see if you can take a sip, without losing yourself to it, without becoming intoxicated. Can you 'hold space' for the witness to what is happening, whatever is being experienced?

This is what Ketu, the opposite lunar node, reflects. Ketu is simply the still witness to all that is apparently happening. From this perspective, nothing is happening; all is.

Become so aware of this 'part' of your being that you are less likely to get triggered. You can taste your poison, but you are not completely under its spell.

Antidotes

There are a number of things you can do to antidote Rāhu if you feel it has become overwhelming in whatever form. But it's important to be mindful of how you approach any remedial measures so as not to use them as crutches or avoidance strategies. No matter how good the remedy, if you're doing it to avoid how you're feeling, what you are experiencing, you're doing yourself a disservice. You may be able to chant a mantra to help your mind cope with the chaos of Rāhu, to bring order, but if you chant with the intention of avoiding the chaos, the chaos will catch up with you. All it takes is an illness or chaotic schedule that scuppers your routine and you're thrown into the intensity of what you've been avoiding. If, on the other hand, you approach any kind of remedial measure with the intention of dealing with the issues, it changes everything. It's a subtle shift in intention, but it makes all the difference.

Much like someone sitting in meditation for hours who fights with themselves with every single breath, you're better off being clear as to what you wish to achieve when meditating. Be honest with yourself about it. And when you slip up and fail to meditate, when the chaos of life seems to take you over, you can still have the meditative experience in the bank, as it were, so you're not as lost. But you're better off finding stillness in the seeming chaos. In other words, the more you can shore up your connection to something beyond what is happening–no matter how chaotic-the more you can stand in that stillness unaffected. And the more you can enjoy Rāhu, too!

The more you identify with the experiencer of the experience, the richer the experience becomes. As Kishori says in our conversations about our "beloved opponent", "Hand on heart." It can be as simple as that.

Hand on Heart

The simple act of placing your hand on your heart is a reminder of the stillness at your centre, in the eye of the storm of Rāhu daśā. Simply placing your hand on your heart allows you to experience stillness in the 'Heartfield', as Kishori puts it. I've practiced this at times when my life has seemed particularly chaotic, when events have challenged me to be centered. It works really well. I've even experienced this spontaneously when being confronted with extremes.

The more extreme the experience, the more profound the stillness.

The experience of chaos itself can make the connection to the stillness of being more profound. And while I don't recommend consciously inviting such chaos into your life to prove a point, it is helpful to be practiced at stilling yourself no matter what is happening.

Rāhu is said to correlate with ultraviolet, which corresponds to the *cakra* or 'wheel of energy' above the crown of the head, while Ketu is said to correlate with infrared, below the root cakra at the base of the pelvic floor. The heart is the centre point between these two extremes. The simple gesture of placing your hand on your heart can be the most profoundly simple technique, a reminder of remaining centred whatever your experience.

Transcending Tamas

Rāhu is *tamas*, one of the three qualities or *guṇas* of Vedic thought that is dark, dull, and unconscious. This is the quality that dominates if you are not doing something to elevate to the other qualities of *rajas* and *sattva*, during Rāhu daśā.

These three qualities, tamas, rajas and sattva, what

could be translated to mean 'inertia', 'activity', and 'harmony', underpin every experience you will ever have. Although you don't want to neglect any of them, many people only catch glimpses of the higher quality of sattva, constantly alternating between tamas and rajas.

While the tamas qualities of dullness, darkness, and unconsciousness are absolutely necessary for the thing you do every day, for maybe eight hours a day, i.e., sleep, if you continue this into your waking day, you may describe your life as the 'living dead'. Yet everyone experiences some level of unconsciousness in Rāhu daśā. Rāhu is a shadow, after all. In its more extreme expressions, its deepest expression of tamas is complete confusion. Rāhu can represent a complete disconnect from reality.

Most of us are somewhat asleep at the wheel in our lives, as it were. Most of us are going about our lives completely unaware of much of what we are doing. And we do so because it's easier to do things unconsciously. Many of the things we do are habit. And while there is nothing wrong with that, as it saves time and energy for the things we must concentrate on, if you are only on autopilot all the time, you are more like the living dead. Rāhu daśā gives you this experience so you can wake up. But waking up suggests you were asleep.

Rāhu daśā shakes you awake many times; through experiences you hadn't consciously planned for. And the potential for Rāhu to offer new perspectives is always there. If you do something completely different, it keeps you out of autopilot mode. It wakes you up. Remember, Rāhu is extreme. It can be extremely unconscious, but also the most awake you've ever been in your life!

Yet you cannot move from a state of tamas, whether a deeper, darker state such as depression, or a 'higher tamas' state of performing tasks habitually, unless you go through a stage of waking up, of agitation. This is rajas.

Rajas is the quality that many of us find ourselves in for a majority of our waking lives. While we may not be asleep during the day, going about our daily activities, we are sort of half asleep, unaware of what we are doing. Activities keep us awake, of course, so we are not completely unconscious when doing something. Rajas is simply activity. Sometimes, it becomes too stimulating but any kind of overstimulation eventually leads to exhaustion, as we slip back down into a state of tamas and fall asleep after a day full of activity.

We may take substances that are more tamas in nature such as alcohol, to help us unwind after a day of being hyperactive. But after a night's sleep induced by alcohol, or perhaps drugs, we need something more to wake us up. We reach for the stimulants to get us going again. On and on it goes, 'highest of highs, lowest of lows'. Except that we are not actually reaching heights of what is possible in the truest sense of the word high. The highs we experience are brief and hard to manage.

They are turbulent and cannot be sustained. And the higher we go, the more we crash.

This is most people's experience of Rāhu daśā. There are often very extreme highs and lows. And don't get me wrong, it's absolutely a lot of fun. But after some years of this, it begins to take its toll. Unless and until you are reaching for the third quality of sattva, a state that is seldom experienced in our modern life, you miss out the one state that is going to help you heal.

Sattva is harmonious, light, and clear. It represents those still moments we all experience between states of hypo- and hyper-activity, i.e., tamas and rajas. But it doesn't occur naturally in Rāhu daśā, as Rāhu's quality is tamas. Tamas can, however, mix with rajas in certain sub-periods to shake things up, and you may indeed find more balance. Rajas helps to balance tamas and is the reason you would seek stimulants or stimulating activities, so you can shake yourself out of being asleep. The problem is you are likely doing so unconsciously.

To incorporate more sattva in your life during Rāhu daśā, you must consciously do so.

Here are a few suggestions to increase sattva naturally. When you wake up, get moving as quickly as possible, preferably outside in the Sun. Move your body and induce a 'natural high'. But do not continue for too long, to the point of exhaustion. That will only, well, exhaust you, sending you into autopilot mode again. Of course, if you didn't sleep well the night before, you haven't incorporated tamas into your life in a healthy way, and it's probably going to spill out into your life during the day, as feelings of lethargy. But you must start somewhere. To do this, you can prioritise your evening routine of winding down and sleeping well, cutting out any stimulants or stimulating activities before bed. Give yourself the best opportunity at restful sleep.

When you wake up after a good night's sleep, take advantage of this by going outside as soon as possible, and, if possible, getting some exercise. Do enough that helps you reach that 'sweet spot', but no more. Then, sit in silence or in meditation for some time. You cannot go from tamas to sattva without a stage of rajas, just as you cannot role out of a deep sleep and sit up in meditation. You know you must move your body and/or breath first.

Another way to increase sattva during your day is to simply take a pause after completing any activity, before moving onto the next. Activities are inherently rajas in quality, and we tend to overdo things, ending up exhausted. But if you take breaks between activities, to simply sit still, you can squeeze more sattva out of your life experience.

This is also why putting your hand on your heart to find stillness is one of the most clarifying experiences. It increase clarity through the quality of sattva.

There are many other ways to increase sattva, but it's important to address one important thing here. Rāhu is naturally more tamas, so you must address the need you have on some level to experience this. To ignore such would be like trying to ignore the seasons; to go about your life as if they didn't exist. You will make life so much easier for yourself if you acknowledge Rāhu daśā as a time when you need to shake things up, to counterbalance the unconscious material that is waking up in you.

While the quality of the shadow is tamas, the reaction to this can either be more tamas or rajas, depending. Observe how you react. Are you trying to numb the experience, to distract yourself in some way? You may use a lot of activities to distract yourself, but it will ultimately lead to exhaustion, to more tamas. You may use even more tamas to check out on some level, which may mean using dulling substances, prescribed or not, if you feel depressed, anxious, or just lost in some way.

As long as you address tamas in a way that acknowledges it, while counterbalancing it to the extent you need, with appropriate activities, all the while increasing the perfect balanced between activity and inactivity, i.e., between rajas and tamas, the more likely you feel well. And yet still, Rāhu daśā can express itself as a sort of perverse part of you that is not interested in being balanced. That too must be acknowledged.

Try not to consciously increase tamas and rajas, at least, as either can lead to more imbalances. There's no point beating yourself up about it. But you *can* do the simple thing of acknowledging your need to shake things up, to shake yourself out of a slumber, while incorporating more balance into your life.

One of the best ways I think that can balance all these needs out in Rāhu daśā is to give your life some sort of framework so you can experience the thrills and spills of Rāhu in a more balanced way. Do something morning and evening that bookends your day, so you can enjoy Rāhu in all its many expressions. Have some sort of ritual you do that contains the chaos that is Rāhu. The more of a framework you have, the more you can enjoy the chaos.

Hand on heart, you can then bring that stillness into the experience.

Rāhu is the experience, but it is not the experiencer. That is represented by Ketu, Rāhu's opposite. The more you can experience the experiencer, in whatever form of practice or ritual you do as often as possible, all day, every day, the more you can still yourself in the apparent chaos.

It could be a walk in nature every morning and evening, for example, or a yoga and meditation practice. It could be a breathing exercise done seated or chanting a mantra. Chanting a mantra (more on this later) is helpful because a mind under Rāhu's spell needs a focus to help it concentrate. If you also chant one that alleviates Rāhu's imbalances, all the better.

Whatever it is you do, see the practice itself as giving your life order, and elevating your energy from the states of tamas, through states of rajas, and finally, lifting yourself up into a state of sattva.

But here's the thing: you don't want to then try to pin down sattva. When Rāhu is involved in such pursuits, it can feel like you're trying to gain enlightenment as just another thing you crave, not realising enlightenment in the truest sense transcends all states of being. Even sattva, no matter how harmonious, is a state. There is something beyond this that silently witnesses all your experiences, through all the different states of being.

This is why someone who is in the deepest, darkest state of tamas, someone who is depressed, can experience an awakening to their true nature beyond form. While it isn't necessarily the typical route, it is possible. Read Eckhart Tolle's description of his awakening in *The Power of Now* (Tolle 2004) and you will see that he was in a state of deep depression for about three years (the length of time of a Saturn sub-period), until his identity crashed, as it were, and he woke up. Most people's experiences are not going to be that dramatic. Most of us attempt to experience awakening by increasing sattva, whether we consciously do so or not. It's far easier to transcend a mind-body that is balanced and peaceful.

But here's the rub: if we do so without realising that even sattva is a state of mind-more closely like a fully awake state of pure being, yes, but still just a state of mind-we may fool ourselves into *thinking* we are awakened. We cannot think ourselves awake.

An awakened being can operate in any state of mind, or experience. The experiencer is what's important, not the experience.

Balancing Vāta

Rāhu is Vāta (windy) in nature, and *tamasic* (leads to inertia). Thus, Rāhu daśā tends to increase the 'wind humour' and usually causes too much or not enough movement. The wind humour is the governing humour and represents 80 classifications of disease according to Āyurveda, the Indian system of health.

Everything moves on Vāta, as movement is the key component of wind. Imbalances of Vāta can show extremes in movement, either too much or not at all; hyper-mental activity and anxiety, or hypo-mental activity and depression. One usually leads to the other. An imbalance of Vāta can alternate between bouts of anxiety and depression. Although these mental states are common to us all, your weak chains may make themselves known to you in more specific ways the more stress you experience. Whether you experience more extreme Vāta imbalances or not, more extreme expresssions of excess or depletion, the stress itself is the trigger.

Rāhu stressors can be enjoyable, of course, but it's important to view them as just that. Too much mental excitement (rajas) or confusion (tamas) can only be experienced for so long before the chain breaks.

Increasing the wind humour can either be a good or bad thing, depending on your constitution, also. If you are more of this humour to begin with, Rāhu daśā is likely to disturb it all the more. Like increases like.

If, on the other hand, you're more of the water humour (Kapha), you may benefit from a shake-up. Rāhu daśā can certainly unsettle, but it can also innovate and make you adapt. This can be a good thing for the water humour individual who tends towards stagnation. Yet too much agitation can have the opposite affect for these people, too. Balance is crucial, as always.

For fire humours (Pitta), Rāhu can certainly be disturbing, as the wind can agitate fire, or even blow it out. The fiery humour individual may feel the need to control outcomes, which can be exaggerated in Rāhu daśā because of the uncertainty, and then suppressed through exhaustion. Rāhu daśā can at least be a little chaotic and difficult to manage, despite the fire humour individual's skills in managing energy. How they deal with this will depend on how much control they think they have. Fire humour individuals should indeed use their skills of energy management, as long as they do not try to wrestle the chaos of Rāhu to the ground. Rāhu daśā requires at least a bit of adaptability because of the oftentimes chaotic changes that are likely.

Vāta individuals need more help with Rāhu daśā. They are the more fearful in general. They are more influenced by Rāhu in the first place. This means that Rāhu is prominently placed in their birth chart, and thus influences their nature and constitution to a larger extent. The mind can only take on so much before it switches off and tunes out. An extreme case of a Vāta imbalance is psychosis. But there are many imbalances that can be experienced on this spectrum.

Whatever constitution you identify with, you may need professional help if the wind humour is particularly imbalanced during Rāhu daśā.

The treatment depends on who is making the diagnosis, of course: a doctor or a priest. One may look at the pathology, while the other may see the awakening that is taking place. I'm not a medical professional so I don't know. The point is that how we label things matters. Some people may need a medical diagnosis to treat an obvious condition, while others may have access to people that know how to manage these kinds of extreme imbalances. We could all do with more sattva, more balance, in our lives no matter who we are.

Alternate Breath

Nādi shodhana, the 'energetic channel cleanse', is achieved through alternate nostril breathing. It's a great antidote to the chaotic energy of Rāhu. By balancing the right and left hemispheres of the brain and 'energy body', you can literally bring yourself into a more balanced state of being in just a few rounds of this breathing technique. You may seek out a teacher to learn it properly, but simply, it's done by gently closing off one nostril at a time and breathing through alternate sides. One round of breath is begun when taking air in through the left nostril, with the right nostril gently closed. Then, closing off the left nostril, exhale through the right. Keeping the right nostril open, inhale through the right, before closing the right and exhaling through the left. This is one round of the breath and is repeated for just a few rounds before increasing the amount you do over time.

Eventually, you can also suspend the breath between inhaling and exhaling, allowing the breath to naturally pause without force. The suspension of the breath, *prāṇāyāma*, is a natural antidote to the chaos of Rāhu. Restraining the breath without strain increases energy throughout your body while instilling calmness in your mind. When the breath is still, the mind is still. Be careful not to strain when doing any kind of breathing exercises. Even if you think you are creating more balance, straining is not a balanced state of being.

By suspending the breath while focusing on balancing the in- and out-breath, you can find more balance and stillness, the two things that are often missing in Rāhu daśā.

Tantrik Yoga

Meditation and physical yoga practices reduce stress due to unexpressed emotions being given a safe space to be felt, healing trauma. These practices can create a safe space to feel what has been suppressed, allowing whatever needs to be revealed in Rāhu daśā to reveal itself safely.

When you meditate or practice physical yoga postures, your 'logical brain' is given a workout and quietens the negative 'emotional brain', the 'reptilian brain' that correlates with Rāhu. When the emotional brain is triggered by stress, it goes into negative overload and is unable to switch it off. The stress system impairs the serotonin, noradrenalin, and dopamine signals, and they become imbalanced. When you practice yoga, you give the logical brain a 'workout' and it quietens the emotional brain.

I must, however, point out a trap that is all too often been my experience in Rāhu daśā in relation to a modern-day yoga practice. Rāhu is not a *yogi*; it's a *bhogi*. This is someone who wants to experience life. If you practice Classical Yoga, which is inherently a path of renunciation for a yogi, you're likely to run into problems at some point during Rāhu daśā, as it's essentially about experiencing the world, i.e., *bhoga*.

You may succeed at wrestling with your shadow's desires and somehow contain them for a time, but you may as well try to convince me you can tame a hurricane for 18 years! Classical Yoga can offer you the discipline you need during Rāhu daśā; but, unless you find your divinity in the world, in yourself, through your shadow, you're likely to be in conflict throughout your Rāhu daśā.

Rāhu is not a part of your being interested in checking out. It's a hidden part of you that is dying to be let loose. Remember, it's 18 years long. There are likely points during its period that you slip and find Rāhu exploding onto the scene in seemingly inappropriate ways. If you've repressed this urge for so long, it's likely to cause you problems as it attempts to break free.

Tantrik Yoga, on the other hand, was developed for those who were not renunciates or ascetics. This is absolutely suitable during Rāhu daśā. The problem with modern-day yoga practices is it's not completely renunciate, nor completely in the world. Instead, it falls between both, in a state of limbo. This is many people's experience of a yoga practice in the modern world, where they do not completely let go of the trappings of the world as they practice a watered-down form of ascetism.

I'm sure you are familiar with this if you practice some form of yoga. You may transcend your pain somewhat, but you do not transcend the world. And because the world causes pain, you end up using yoga as a means to cope. But you have stayed where the pain was, and is, formed-in the world. You may sometimes experience release in meditation, but once it's over, you're back in the 'real world' again. It helps, of course, but it is not an awakened state of being. It's only partial.

Tantra is not about denying anything, even if it's painful. It's about using whatever to awaken to your true nature. And while Classical Tantra is not just about sex, nothing is off the table. It's not about the activity, it's about using whatever activity to awaken.

Tantra is about cultivating energy. You can incorporate this into your yoga practice in the form of practices that make you feel more alive. But herein lies the problem. When you approach a path which is actually about renunciation (Classical Yoga), you may end up feeling better due to a practice that renounces the world. You are attempting to renounce what makes you feel better. You feel better in a body that you are attempting to transcend.

For years, I struggled with this dilemma, because I didn't understand the distinction. Once you figure it out, your yoga practice, whatever the form, will be sublime. You will relax into your being, into the moment, without struggling with contradictory paths often mixed up in a modern yoga practice.

You don't have to change *what* you are doing, only the *way* you approach it. Tantra is not about trying to remove anything. It's not about becoming something else, although this will occur in its own good time with practice. This is the crux of Rāhu daśā.

Another issue with modern-day yoga practices is they don't always address the individual's needs based on their energy levels. Rāhu daśā can already be quite taxing on one's energy. The needs of someone in this daśā are different to someone who is full of energy. Simply, if you are stressed and you practice a form of yoga that depletes your energy stores, you are likely to feel worse over time, not better. It may give temporary relief, but too much rajas, too much activity, leads to more tamas.

Rāhu daśā already has enough tamas. There is no need for more. Cultivate more sattva and more balance through appropriate levels of exercise. Always look for the 'sweet spot' in anything you do. If you are particularly stressed, practice more gentle, restorative exercises to help counteract the depletion. You still need some rajas to wake up the tamas in you, but only just enough so that you don't slip back down into tamas. This is the same for any kind of physical activity, be it running, cycling, whatever. You may wish to overcome any nervous energy and confusion with these exercises, but don't confuse being at peace with being exhausted. Don't confuse sattva with tamas. Someone who is exhausted may look like they are at peace from the outside. But exhaustion is an experience of emptiness, of depletion. Sattva is an experience of fullness, of stillness, of being at peace.

The Tantrik approach will make your practice a richer experience, whatever you do. If you decide you are not going to renounce the world, but allow the world to exist in you, as you, you awaken to your divinity. This is the path of Rāhu daśā.

Planets as Antidotes

Jupiter is one of the best antitodes during Rāhu daśā, just as generosity is the best remedy for greed. However, if Jupiter were too close to Rāhu's shadow, either in your birth chart or by transit, it too can feel overshadowed, reflected in a lack of discernment. In that case, remedial measures to enhance the Sun can bring more clarity.

Gratitude, an expression of Jupiter, is something to cultivate during Rāhu daśā to counteract its negative impulses. Though the tendency during Rāhu daśā is to measure yourself from where you are to where you want to be, making you feel unfulfilled, you can always measure yourself from where you've come from. When you do that, you may realise you have achieved so much in Rāhu daśā. Yet still, without being grateful for what you have, right now, you're unlikely to be happy with where you find yourself.

With greed, you want more. With gratitude, you are content with what you have. You happen to get more with gratitude than greed, anyway. The very hunger for something is the thing that prevents you getting it, as if trying to grasp something itself squeezes the life out of it. Trying too hard is the best way to guarantee you don't get it. When you give thanks, you have more and more to give. When you are generous, it's sending you a message that you have more than enough-and you get more than enough.

Jupiter represents beingness, which antidotes
Rāhu's tendency to project you into the future, allowing
you to be in the present, where everything you want
actually is. It allows you to simply be. Acknowledging
that you have everything you want gets you out of the
fight, flight, or freeze mode. It gets you out of the low-
or high-level alert mode so you can rest in pure being,
where everything is given to you, anyway.

Saturn is another planet whose significations can
antidote Rāhu, by 'grounding' you in what is real. Rāhu
is unreal, including unreal expectations. And while
being unreal allows you to see beyond what is presented
as reality, where you can innovate, if this impulse is
taken too far, you may simply experience life as an
'unreality', completely disconnected from what is
happening around you. Focus on what is real in your
life. Be with it. Make reality your friend. Then you can
evolve more easily.

Know the rules of the game, the game of life. You
cannot begin to break rules in Rāhu daśā unless you are
one with them. Rāhu daśā involves at least a little bit of
tweaking or bending the rules to suit your special needs.

Another way Saturn can antidote Rāhu is through
the air element, which both Saturn and Rāhu represent.
Saturn co-rules the air sign Aquarius along with Rāhu.
Breathing exercises or prāṇāyāma (breath control) is a
powerful tool to antidote Rāhu's chaotic tendencies.
Simply being aware of your breath is one of the most
grounding, and real, experiences you can have. Adding

more control, more restraint to the breath, actually creates more energy in your body, and more focus for the mind. Breathing rhythmically helps regulate your system, and another way Saturn antidotes Rāhu, but also brings in the light and energy of the Sun.

The Sun represents rhythm, health, and vitality. It is incorporated through rhythmic movements such as exercise and dance. Music is another signification for the Sun, uplifting the heart and mind through rhythmic movements-another great antitode to Rāhu.

Simply being more aware of your physical form, especially if you exist in an online or virtual world, can do wonders to balance Rāhu's tendency to focus your awareness solely in your head. For this reason, Ketu is one of the best antidotes to Rāhu, i.e, being in your body, sensing, feeling what is happening, getting you out of your head.

Wearing virtual reality headsets or other wearable technologies is likely to increase as we enter the Age of Aquarius. This is an expression of the head of the demon in Vedic myth, overly focusing on being in your head, literally. Being more grounded in what is real, in your breath, in your body, in tune with nature all around you, becomes all the more important in the Aquarian Age, especially while also experiencing Rāhu daśā.

The Black Sun

Psychiatrists Barry Michels and Phil Stutz offer tools to better manage your shadow. Their book, *Coming Alive* (Michels & Stutz 2017), describes visualisations that help you deal with Rāhu, what they call "Part X." One of the tools is called "The Black Sun", a visualisation you can use when you feel a craving for something that zaps your "Life Force." They describe four stages of the visualisation: *deprivation*, *emptiness*, *fullness*, and *giving*.

Deprivation asks you to feel the yearning for something when it arises as intensely as you can. *Emptiness* asks you to be at one with the void. This is a reminder of Ketu, the south node. By being at one with the void, you realise that the void is full of everything. Your awareness of emptiness becomes an experience of *fullness*, the third part of the visualisation. This step asks you to visualise a "Black Sun" ascending inside you, expanding until you become one with it. The final step of *giving* asks you to turn your attention to the outside world, visualizing the Black Sun becoming a "pure white light of infinite giving." This is an apt analogy and visualization of what happens during an eclipse of the Sun. As the shadows pass, the light returns. After Rāhu daśā ends, the 'inner light' of Jupiter fills you. The fuller you feel, the more you can give. By giving more, even during Rāhu daśā, you are given more to give.

As they describe the tool on their website, "When Part X [Rāhu] is tempting you to give in to your impulses, what it's trying to do is steal your Life Force. Self-restraint not only preserves your Life Force, it increases it. When you hold an impulse back, the lower, greedy energy is transformed into a higher, giving energy, increasing your Life Force."

Ketu Mantras

Mantras are an extremely helpful practice for Rāhu daśā because the mind may be too unsettled to sit quietly. Sometimes the mind needs an extra focus, such as a mantra, breath, and/or a visualisation. Mantras offer both the sounding of the words and the regulation of the breath. An especially useful mantra to begin with is one for Gaṇeśa, the 'remover of obstacles'-the obstacle being Rāhu. The mantra *Om Gaṃ Gaṇapataye Namaḥ* is a simple yet effective one to begin with. When you see an 'ā' sound in Sanskrit, it is more like the English a, as in the word 'apple', whereas when you see an 'a' sound without a dash, it is sounded more like 'uh', or the beginning sound in the word 'orange'. Think apples and oranges!

There is a rule within the Gaṇeśa mantra, as the seed mantra for Gaṇeśa, GAṂ is followed with a 'ga' sound. Instead of sounding GAṂ with an 'm' sound to the lips, the 'm' sound is made at the back of the throat and ends up sounding like 'gan' or 'gong'. This is why you often see this mantra written as *Om Gong Gaṇapataye Namaḥ* or *Om Gan Gaṇapataye Namaḥ*.

The word *Namaḥ* brings up a controversy surrounding what is called the *visarga* sound at the end of the word, with a dot under the letter 'h'. Although many Sanskrit scholars say an echo of the preceding vowel should be sounded, which would mean it is sounded as *namaha*, others say it should not be sounded, and that the visarga merely represents a release of the breath. This release of breath is compared to that of a baby snake, a faint release and not an audible sounding. No such controversy exists if the word namaḥ were found in the middle of a mantra, such as *Om Namaḥ Śivāya*, where everyone agrees that the extra sound is left out.

You could also chant the name of Gaṇeśa based on Ketu in your birth chart. The following are the mantras for each form of Gaṇeśa in each zodiac sign, where the mantra huṁ (pronounced hoom) is added to each.

Aries	vakratuṇḍāya huṁ
Taurus	ekadantāya huṁ
Gemini	kṛṣṇapiṅgākṣāya huṁ
Cancer	gajavaktrāya huṁ
Leo	lambodarāya huṁ
Virgo	vitaṭāya huṁ
Libra	vighnarājāya huṁ
Scorpio	dhūmravarṇāya huṁ
Sagittarius	bhālacandrāya huṁ
Capricorn	vināyakāya huṁ
Aquarius	gajapataye huṁ
Pisces	gajānanāya huṁ

There is another, more specific way, to use the above mantras. Find the planet that rules the 11th sign of your birth chart if you have a movable rising sign (ascendant), i.e., Aries, Cancer, Libra or Capricorn; the 9th sign ruling planet if you have a fixed sign rising, i.e., Taurus, Leo, Scorpio or Aquarius, or the 7th sign ruling planet if you have a dual sign rising, i.e., Gemini, Virgo, Sagittarius, or Pisces. See where the planet that rules this sign is placed in your birth chart and chant the mantra for the sign opposite, using the Ketu mantra for the sign given. This method is a more specific way to remove the Rāhu blocks you are likely to experience.

Durgā Mantra

Durgā is the deity most associated with Rāhu. The 'dark goddess' and 'fierce feminine' deity can be invoked as a means to quickly remove the problems of Rāhu, especially if the mind has become particularly agitated.

Durgā mantras are said to be best chosen by the individual, as opposed to most other mantras which are prescribed. Approach the goddess with an open heart and see what mantra you feel drawn to. One mantra for Durgā is *Oṁ Hrīṁ Śrīṁ Klīṁ Durgati-nāśinyai Mahāmāyāyai svāhā*. This is translated by Freedom Cole as meaning, "Oṁ triple formed Goddess, who is the Great Illusion, destroy my bad direction, so be it" (Cole 2023). You may feel drawn to another Durgā mantra. Whatever mantra you choose, you can invoke the goddess to quickly clear your blocks.

Mrtyuñjaya Mantra

Mrtyuñjaya is a very special mantra to help you overcome fear. It is chanted for Śiva, 'the destroyer', a deity that can help with Rāhu. It is a powerful remedy to overcome illness, even the fear of death. Chanting it every morning and evening for forty days is said to bring healing, and a healer, if needed. It is a powerful tool to have during Rāhu daśa.

Oṃ tryambakaṃ yajāmahe sugandhiṃ puṣṭivardhanam urvārukamiva bandhanān mṛtyor mukṣīya mā'mṛtāt

Sanjay Rath translates the mantra in *Vedic Remedies in Astrology* (Rath, 2000): "O! Three-eyed Lord Shiva (three luminous eyes represent the Sun, Moon and Holy fire) we worship Thee; Thy (name and fame) spreads like sweet fragrance as Thou art the savior of all beings. I am under the bondage of dreadful diseases (of the mind, body and soul) and pray that Thou shalt deliver us from (all evils including) death (for the sake of immortality) by granting us some life rejuvenating nectar."

The sounds of the Sanskrit words correspond to their meaning. The word *yajāmahe*, for example, captures its meaning: 'we sing thy praise'. The word *bandhanān* gives a sense of being 'bound down'.

196

The Headless Way

The Headless Way (headless.org) are a series of "experiments" that awaken you to who you really are. They open you to the experience of a 'non-self', the experiencer of the experience, the witness, or observer. Whatever name you give it, 'it' is not something; rather, the experiencer of the thing.

I was reintroduced to the experiments during my own Rāhu-Ketu daśā, appropriately enough. I was first introduced to them some years before, but they didn't grab me at the time. As soon as I began my Ketu sub-period, I found them to be the key to unlocking the profound truths of Ketu in an immediate way. I can only describe the 'experience' as an awakening, but it was not something grand as I had been taught to believe it would be. At the same time, it was the most profound 'experience' of my life.

The experiments themselves are so simple that you may wonder why it's not more complicated to awaken. And therein lies the problem. We are taught by some spiritual teachers that it's *going to* take a lot of work to awaken, that it's *going to* take years. But the truth is it's another way Rāhu blocks. You might say, this is the biggest block and deceit of Rāhu. It tricks you into thinking you cannot awaken to the truth of who you really are. It's a trick of the mind, a mind that is projected into the future. When the mind wants something it perceives is in the future, it cannot have it, now. And awakening to the truth of who you really are can only happen now.

Ketu represents our origins; our true nature; our essence being, which is pure awareness without the interference of the mind and its attachments-even our attachments to how we think an awakening should occur.

The experiments of *The Headless Way* were originally given by philosopher Douglas Harding, and now led by Richard Long. They awaken you without years of struggling with your mind. They tap you into the void at your center, beyond mind, instantaneously. You become aware of the still point at your center with all of life's experiences arising and falling within that stillness. You are awareness itself. The awakening to this truth is instantaneous and does not require hours of meditation to achieve. You can simply become aware while performing any activity and remember who you really are. Your head is replaced with what you are observing. Everything opens up. Rāhu is completely obliterated.

All of this begs the question: What or who are we at our core? We are nothing but the capacity for experience, it seems. If you move deeper and deeper into who you are, what you really are is simply a void in which experience arises. At a certain distance you are the you that you most identify with. Your gender, name, status, etc. (Rāhu). But if you go closer and closer, you begin to see yourself as tissues, cells, molecules, and atoms ... and then nothing - empty space (Ketu). Ketu represents that nothingness which is actually full of everything. Ketu is your true nature and where you came from. Yes, you came from a void and anything which you identify with in your body and mind, will one day return to that void. To have an experience of this void is to be empty for experience; to be fully open for life experience but firmly rooted in awareness. The relief that is felt from such revelations is immeasurable, especially in the midst of Rāhu daśā.

Get Organised!

If there were just one piece of advice I could give to someone starting out in Rāhu daśā, it would be to get organised. The more organised you can be, the less Rāhu's chaos causes problems. Instead, you can take the ingenuity of Rāhu and apply it to your growth. And because growth cannot happen unless there is some organisation, the more organised you can be, the better. This is the biggest rub of Rāhu daśā: the more you want, the less you get, because the excess is unmanageable. Although Rāhu is the catalyst for growth in the first place, it must be balanced with being more organised if you are to experience growth.

When people tell me about their 'kuṇḍalinī awakening', I think of the initial disorganization that occurs and shakes them up. Yet herein lies a distinction from pure being and awareness I must point out.

Kuṇḍalinī śakti is an energy; and this kind of energy, just like Rāhu, can be too volatile for a lot of people to manage. Beingness is the awareness of what is, and not about cultivating or transforming energy from one state to another. And this is why it's especially important to be mindful of how you approach these kinds of energy practices during Rāhu daśā. They may be hard to manage. Yet *kuṇḍalinī śakti* may indeed get triggered in Rāhu daśā without your conscious provocation, and you must deal with it. In that case, I recommend getting an expert tantrika as a guide, someone who can advise about kuṇḍalinī and how to manage it.

If you've had a 'kuṇḍalinī awakening' and you're finding your energy is harder to manage, I would at least recommend framing your days with some sort of discipline. Give yourself some sort of framework to be able to enjoy the revelations. Regulate your system as much as you can, without trying to tie down the beast that is Rāhu if it has already been let loose from its cage. Instead, give it a bigger cage!

While you may not identify with a kuṇḍalinī awakening, you *are* awakening in Rāhu daśā. Best not to awaken the beast before it is ready to emerge naturally.

Get an Astrology Reading

Having an astrologer look at the specifics of your birth chart can help you focus on your particular blind spots that block you from getting what you want. But just knowing something about your blind spots doesn't remove them. You must take this knowledge and do something with it. If you find an astrologer is *only* positive or *only* negative about Rāhu, run a mile! If someone is only positive about an experience you know to be more challenging, you'll think there is something wrong with you and they haven't acknowledged it. There's nothing wrong with you. You have a shadow just like they do. The astrologer may not be willing to look at their own, and thus, yours. If someone is only negative about Rāhu, this is equally divisive and unhelpful. It further cuts parts of you off by demonizing your shadow, which they are just as likely to wish to avoid. They may be unwilling to look at their own in any positive light.

Get a reading with an astrologer who has been through 18 years of Rāhu daśā or has studied it in great depth; ideally, both.

If you would like to book a reading with me, go to timelineastrology.com.

Afterword

I trust my insights into Rāhu daśā have been helpful. If I have left anything out, let us give Rāhu its due. There must be something left in the shadows, shadows which are never removed, only incorporated into what it means to be a human being. I know being more conscious of anything is helpful, so having more awareness of your 'shadow period' should be no different. But I also know it's important to go with Rāhu daśā to a degree, to let it unfold as it will, while managing it as best you can.

Try not to beat yourself up about it. It's all happening perfectly. Actually, nothing happens; all is. Let that be a mantra for when things don't seem to go to plan. The other option of trying to ignore it may bring unintended consequences. Not acting is an action.

Whether you overthink it and are paralyzed or you don't think at all, you may you end up somewhere you didn't seem to intend. Just being open to the ideas in this book will help you move forward, no matter how uncertain you feel.

Finally, let me leave you with a few suggestions to help you thrive in Rāhu daśā:

- Ask how you can better live as a unique individual within your society and global community.

- Do for others what you would like for yourself. Give to others what you want. If you don't have it to give, help the other get what you both want. Greed is a one-way street, which easily gets clogged without give and take.

- Address your shadow. The more you can see the other as yourself, the better off you'll be- and everyone else, too.

- Recognise that your primitive brain and survival instincts are mostly inappropriate in a modern context. Watching horrific scenes on a screen, whether real or fictional, requires you to do something with the stress induced.

- Use rituals to keep the waywardness of Rāhu at bay. Rāhu needs some sort of organisation, to contain and make sense of the insightful, yet chaotic, input.

- If you need an organisation or a professional therapist to help you organise your thoughts, seek help. You are not alone, no matter how much you may think you are.

- Put your hand on your heart. Kishori says a mind rooted in the "heartfield" is without conflict. It is far more effective at getting what it wants, too.

- Be in your life, moment-to-moment, as much as you can.

Auṁ Tat Sat

Bibliography

Cole, F. (n.d.). *Durgā Mantras* – Freedom Vidya. [online] Available at: https://shrifreedom.org/vedic-astrology/mantra/12749-2/ [Accessed 31 Jan. 2023].

Egan, D. (2017). *Is This the Age of Aquarius?* [online] Astrology News Service. Available at: https://astrologynewsservice.com/articles/is-this-the-age-of-aquarius/ [Accessed 31 Jan. 2023].

Lama, B.P. (n.d.). *Rahu the Dragons Head - * BP Lama Jyotishavidya*. [online] Available at: https://barbarapijan.com/bpa/Graha/Rahu/1Rahu_Mai nPage.htm. [Accessed 31 Jan. 2023].

Michels, B. and Stutz, P. (2017). *Coming Alive*. London: Penguin Random House.

Rath, S. (2000). *Vedic Remedies in Astrology*, New Delhi: Sagar Publications.

Schulman, M. (1977). *Karmic Astrology*. York Beach, Me: Samuel Weiser.

Sharma, G.C. (2006). *Brihat Parasara Hora Sastra* Volume 1. New Delhi: Sagar Publications.

Subramanya, S. V. (2008). *Vaidyanatha Dikshita's Jataka Parijata*, vol. III. New Delhi: Ranjan Publications.

Tolle, E. (2004). *The Power of NOW: A Guide to Spiritual Enlightenment*. Vancouver, B.C.: Namaste Publishing.

Wilber, K. (2018). *Doshin asks Ken Wilber about Shadows*. [online] Available at: https://www.youtube.com/watch?v=T_lxS_blPvM [Accessed 31 Jan. 2023].

About the Author

Gary O'Toole has studied astrology since 1996, specialising in Jyotiṣa (Vedic astrology). His first book, *Cosmic Bodies,* explored the relationship between Āyurveda and Jyotiṣa. His latest, *Daśā Vidyā,* delves into timing techniques from India.

He writes a blog for patrons and produces a magazine, podcast, and online learning platform. His readings impart an empowered view of the timeline of your life, available at timelineastrology.com.

Acknowledgments

Thank you to all my patrons, students, and clients over the years. You have probably taught me more than I you. A special thank you to Douglas Gould for feedback on the first draft. Some of the chapters were adapted from articles I wrote for the *Timeline Astrology* website and magazine.

Thank you to my astrology teacher Pearl Finn; and to Jeanette 'Kishori' McKenzie for her unique approach to Rāhu, our "Beloved opponent." Our conversations on the *Timeline Astrology Podcast* have added invaluable perspectives.